# An Intellectual in Khaki

# An Intellectual in Khaki

Dr Bhupendra Kumar Singh & Sapna Pathania

KALPAZ

ISBN: 978-93-5128-198-6

Price: ₹ 225

First Published, 2016

*Published by*

Kalpaz Publications
C-30, Satyawati Nagar,
Delhi – 110052
E-mail: kalpaz@hotmail.com
Ph.: 9212142040

*Printed at:* G. Print Process, Delhi

**Cataloging in Publication Data—DK**
Courtesy: D.K. Agencies (P) Ltd. <docinfo@dkagencies.com>

**Pathania, Bhupendra Kumar Singh Sapna, author.**
An intellectual in Khaki / Dr Bhupendra Kumar Singh Sapna Pathania.
pages cm
ISBN 9789351281986

1. Chauhan, Sharad Satya, 1968- 2. Police—India—Biography. I. Title.

HV7911.C43P38 2016 DDC 363.2092 23

**Our humble efforts are dedicated to**

*All the Men in Khaki including those of the Central Police Forces who have endeared the nation by their devotion to duty and self-less sacrifice to ensure life, dignity, honour and safety to all of us.*

# Contents

# Introduction

The intellect is the most potent gift endowed by the nature to mankind. It is not that other lowly creatures do not have an intellect, but at best, it is very rudimentary and helps the animal world only for the purposes of procreation and to develop their survival instincts. It is only in the human race which by virtue of the precious gift of nature we call mind not only creates sustains growth and material opulence and also tames a hostile environment around him for the enrichment of civilisation and culture.

The potency of the intellect is twofold. It can be positive in the form of a creative energy responsible for our survival and growth but at the same time it can be negative, which is destructive. The long list of wars recorded in our history have resulted in the loss of millions of human lifes and wastage of human resources bear ample testimony to this fact.

We are conscious of the fact that we may be targeted by cynical minds and invite criticism for our tearing hurry to author the biography of an officer who has just started his career. In our defence, we would say that Dronacharya, the great teacher of the siblings of the Kuru dynasty in the Mahabharat period was the first biographer of the world. In those ancient times the spoken word enjoyed more credibility and authenticity than the written word. He was the biographer of his own disciple Arjun concluded his oral biography of his young student by saying that his disciple Arjun would be the best archer in the world.

We are fully aware of the fact that excellence or accomplishments are relative terms and in due course of time fade away into insignificance. That is the reason of our hurry. Our sole intention is to bring forth the situations, circumstances, tribulations, failures, frustrations and mysteries of human behaviour as we analyse his personality before these are lost or obliterated in the whirlpool of time.

The personality of Dr Sharad Satya Chauhan an IPS officer of 1992 batch always fascinated us. We were always at a loss to understand as to how an individual who had such a bright medical career ahead of him could jettison this creative profession and choose an alternative which according to our thinking was a tougher option. In our efforts to present a pen-picture of the officer in the shape of a biography, we have sailed miles away from his professional profile. The reasons for so doing was the fact that we were conscious of our limitations as it called for an altogether different type of mind set and expertise to judge his professional profile. Further, we did not want our effort to be branded as a compendium of the annual confidential reports earned by the officer. To decipher the mystery of why he choose the thorns and not the roses was itself very challenging. To our utter surprise, the answers to our curiosity was lying scattered around us in the open. The primary reason was his intellectual bent of mind and having full faith on his intellectual propensities he chose the difficult but challenging option.

We are thankful to Air Cmdr Ajay Singh Pathania VSM, a Helicopter Pilot and an alumni of Defence Services Staff College Wellington (Tamil Nadu) who has been trained in the Anti Terrorism operations in Australia and in the United States for his valuable suggestions and guidance in military matters. Thanks to Late Dr (Smt) Mithlesh Singh, mother of the policeman. Though very reticent by nature, she was always graceful and virtually opened the floodgates of valuable inputs to us, which we could have never gathered from any other source. Our thanks are also due to Smt Vishal Chauhan, the wife of the policeman. Though docile and unassuming in temperament she is always a pillar of strength for her husband and provided the forceful motivation to Sharad to indulge in the luxury of intellectual pursuits. The story of Sharad Chauhan, who by his sheer grit and determination negotiated numerous road blocks in persuit of his intellectual goals, would definitely inspire our youth who are ambitions and talented as well. In reality, it is our sole intention to put across to the coming generation that with a steady mind, belief in one self, hard work and dedication, any goal can be achieved in life.

**Dr Bhupinder Singh and Sapna Pathania**

Maha Shivratri 17th Feb. 2015

# Chapter I

# There is Something in a Name

It was Sunday, the 3rd March 1968 when Sharad was born in Kamala Nehru Hospital at Allahabad. It may take many by surprise since the parents of the new born did not belong to this city. His mother was a Rajput girl of Sombanshi clan from Pratapgarh and his father a Chauhan from Banda (now Chitrakoot) district, both in Uttar Pradesh. To orient with the facts, it is imperative to peep further deep into the past history of the families to understand the factor leading to the matrimonial bondage to achieve the true perspective.

Sombanshis are a high class Rajput clan, mostly inhabiting the Pratapgarh and Hardoi belt between the rivers Ganga and Yamuna. It is proudly said about them that you will never find either a poor Sombanshi or an extraordinarily rich, one. They never borrow money from anyone as they are very frugal in their life style. There are historical reasons for such characteristies. It is a matter of record that during the first war of Indian Independence of 1857 which British historians call Indian Mutiny, 50 per cent of the individuals who were sent to the gallows for their overt participation in the mutiny in UP were Sombanshi their contribution to the independence effort. It was therefore natural for the British to keep them under control and ensure that they were never allowed to prosper economically. In contrast, the Chauhans of the paternal side of Sharad had an altogether diametrically opposite background.

*With Mother when 1½ Years Old*

*With Sister Sapna Pathania the co-author of the Biography*

It appears that in the later part of the seventeenth century; they left their homeland around the erstwhile Jodhpur state and migrated to UP as mercenaries in search of greener pastures. They annexed a part of the area from the Chandel rulers and established a small principality called Asothar in Fatehpur district of UP. They had an insatiable urge to expand. With swords and spears a few of them therefore migrated to Banda District. Owing to their migratory character, they became adept in exploiting the local political scenario to their best advantage. During the 1857, in close coordination with the local chieftains of the neighbouring area, they planned a loot, the Maratha treasury in Karwi to plunder wealth. It may be stated that Karvi (now Chitrakoot) was a part of the Maratha kingdom ruled from present day Jhansi. As they found the British there, they instantly changed their colour like a lizard and sent a missionary to the British officers to convince them that they were friends and had come to offer their unstinted cooperation. The British were mighty pleased with such unsolicited support that they amply rewarded them in due course. The Chauhans got three villages of zamindari along with other leaders of the campaign. Many may not be able to accept this story but we have very authentic information that Tikait Singh Chauhan who migrated to Arki sometime before 1857, had only one bullock to plough his agricultural lands. He used to borrow somebody's bullock. The system is still found in vogue in villages with poor farmers and the arrangement is a called PONDAKA i.e. sharing with someone to plough the fields. It was simply a jackpot for them without shedding a drop of sweat or blood.

Apparently acquiring the status of a landlord opened the floodgates of opulence for the family. No wonder the grandfather of Sharad, Harpal Singh was sent to Udai Pratap College, Varanasi, and his elder brother Mahavir Singh to Balwant Rajput College, Agra, for studies. In the early twentieth century, whereas the Mayo College, Ajmer, catered for the education of the princes, these two schools were prestigious educational institutions for the children of the landlord community in the Hindi belt. It may not be out of place to mention that Mahendra Singh, a class fellow of Mahavir Singh, in BR college, Agra, is the father of Vijay Raje Scindia, the ex-maharani of Gwalior. History unfolds in a very strange way. After graduation, Mahendra Singh was nominated as the then prevailing practice, as a Doputs, Collector, who, by yet another strange twist of history, married the daughter of the famous Rana family of Nepal. Their family was expelled by the King of Nepal and had taken refuge in India.

During the British rule, the Principals of the BR College, Agra, and UP College, Varanasi, who used to be British had the prerogative to nominate two students as sub-inspectors of Police in Uttar Pradesh thus both the brothers were appointed Police Sub Inspectors in the early twentieth century. Thus, two out of the three brothers got a job without having ever applied for the same, a rare honour in late 1920's. It may however be mentioned, that it was not easy to get a High School Certificate, since notwithstanding the marks in the written examination, one had to clear an English dictation test. Obviously, the native students were found deficient in comprehending the spoken language dictation by a British examiner, and it invariably took a few years to clear the examination. We understand the police

Sub-Inspector was the highest functionary of the police force in those days and this method was very effective for the British rulers to communicate with an illiterate local population. The appointment in the Police Department did not interest the two; hence both the brothers took voluntary retirement in 1942 and 1947 respectively; much before India got independence, there purpose was to look after their Zamindari, which to them, appeared more glamorous, to the police job. The Zamindar System was abolished in 1953 leaving them with not even a tiny strip of land in their possession. They fell into a deep financial crisis. Narration of this background is essential to understand how the two family's miles apart in their thinking and attitudes, got into a matrimonial alliance. In science we have studied that like poles repel and the unlike poles attract. This phenomenon explains best how the families came together and bonded well with each other in the years to come.

After abolition of the Zamindari in 1953, the family had as they did not have agricultural land. To control the damage and overcome the financial crisis, all the gold ornaments of the ladies were sold and Sharad's grandfather purchased approximately 150 acres of agricultural land. To put the financial recovery on track, a diesel pump which used to be imported from England, in those days, was also purchased, it cost the astronomical amout of Rs 2700. This was more than the cost of a Jeep in 1955. Nothing worked smoothly since this pump was moody and hardly functional and rarely worked satisfactorily. It worsened the financial crisis further.

The family from a shallow pit fell into the deep well of financial crisis. The studies of the eldest son who had just completed his graduation from Agra University came to a halt. The other son who had just completed his plus two examination, had to be sent to DAV College Kanpur for further studies. The old tradition of extravagance just to satisfy the ego of past status, unwarranted habits of meddling in other's affairs continued unabatedly causing undue financial strain with the result, the family never came close to the path of economic recovery.

The financial crisis took a huge toll on the education of the children Mahendra Pratap Singh, who graduated in 1953, had to take up a job of Rs 40 per month as an English teacher in a junior high school. The most humiliating factor was that he had to start his career as a very low paid employee in the village where he was married. Another son, Satya Pratap Singh had to pull out from college because there was nobody to pay his college fees. His father's meagre pension of Rs 57 per month was too little for household expenses let alone meeting the expenses of education of the children. He also found it to be physically too taxing to walk about 15 kilometers every day from Sisa Mau Bazar to Green Park where the college was located. In any case, daily life was too humiliating since he was lodging and boarding as a non-paying guest at his sister's residence. Frustrated as he was, he took a plunge and stood in a queue where the selection for the recruitment in the Indian Navy was taking place. Fortunately, he was the sole individual selected out of the crowd of over five hundred job seekers on that day. In retrospect, it appears to be a big achievement, as it has become very competitive today to be selected as a soldier in the army or state constabulary. Since he was still a minor, being only 16 years of age, he was taken as a trainee boy at a monthly stipend of Rs 27 per month. The remuneration was less than the amount a worker tilling their agricultural land in his village got. His educational background by those days was very high and he was selected as a worthy candidate, and dispatched to the battle cruiser INS Mysore as a trainee officer for the Indian Navy.

During this period, a war of short duration broke out when India decided to liberate Goa from the Portuguese rule. INS Mysore was tasked to capture ANJU DIV Island in the Arabian Sea off Warship Coast in Karnataka. Seeing the Indian warship the Portuguese army occupying the island hoisted the white flag of surrender. Captain SFJ Cameron of the ship decide to pulverise the target before dispatching the landing party he was over ruled by the Admiral who was Commanding the fleet. He was flying his flag on board INS Mysore as an overall Commander of the component Naval of the war. The result was that the naval landing party was welcomed with heavy machine gun fire, inspite of the white flag indicating their surrender. One sailor, who was crawling to the target, along with Satya Pratap Singh, was instantly killed, besides few others were also killed by machine gun fire. The remnants of the landing party were therefore withdrawn and the enemy defensive positions were razed to the ground by the pounding of the heavy guns of the ship. A fresh landing party was sent, and the target captured. The death of his colleague, acted as a catalyst to the poetic instincts of Singh, and he wrote an elegy in memory of Shyam Singh, his departed friend. His poem was adjudged the best poem of the in-house magazine 'VARUNA' and awarded a cheque of Rs 25 by the Hon Chief of the Naval Staff. It was the month of December in 1961 and it was really a fortune for a creative effort even by today's standards. The real gain was, that a poet was born in Singh even after Singh refused to learn the lessons of life, and still continues to indulge in writing poems in pursuit of achieving an elusive goal of becoming a poet. His naval career was doomed because of the spat between the Admiral and Captain of the ship. None of the candidates of his batch got a commission in the Indian Navy. The invasion by the Chinese army into India in 1962, however, opened yet another window for Singh. A large number of young people were granted an emergency commission in the Army. Singh was commissioned in the regiment of Jammu and Kashmir Rifles. It is a prestigious regiment. This regiment earned two Param Vir Chakras in a single battle and also the tag of the bravest of the brave in Kargil war in 1998. The role of the regiment was equally praiseworthy in the 1965 and 1971 wars. So it was in 1967 that the Sombanshis selected this young and dashing Captain of the Army and gave away their educated and accomplished daughter's hand in June 1967 to Capt. Singh with uncertain career prospects.

The Sombanshis were not guided by any immediate gain but definitely had a vision even in such a scenario. It was to this couple a son Saral was born in March 1968. Definitely the Sombanshi had clarity in their vision. They were fully conscious of the fact that in spite of the infinite expanse of the sky it was only the mother earth which had the attributes to create and it was this conviction and faith in the unquestionable capabilities of their daughter, that they entered into an unequal matrimonial alliance with the Chauhans. But how such confidence took the shape of a reality is yet another interesting story.

The person who was instrumental in bringing the two families together was Daryao Singh; a forgotten class fellow of Singh, he was the son of a landlord of Pahari village in Banda district. He was a law graduate of Allahabad University, who gave up his flourishing law practice. He found the profession of law distasteful to his philosophy of life. He could never reconcile to the fact that he would have to take briefs of scheming and manipulative persons to present a distorted and untrue picture to the honourable courts to earn his bread. He thus diverted his expertise and energies to the well being of the society at large. To fix the marriage of his ungrateful friend was his agenda and he exhibited extraordinary zeal and succeeded too. Daryao was a very soft spoken man and always spoke in whispering tone which gave credibility to his arguments in any serious negotiations.

The match was not going very smoothly on the bridegroom's side as father of the boy, to the utter astonishment of his kin-folk, declared that he would not allow the family priest to solemnise the marriage and declared that he would himself conduct the ceremony as enshrined in the Vedic scriptures. To him, Bacchu Pandit, the family priest, was no match to the scholarly priest present on the bride's side. It is -

inconceivable as to have achieved proficiency in Sanskrit language besides Persian even while serving in the Police Dept for over twenty five years. We are however witness to the fact that he was a voracious reader and used to study and also recite Valmiki Ramayan, Adhyatm Ramayan and Shrimad Bhagwat, all textbooks in Sanskrit; and translate the contents thereof to the devotees who gathered around him in the evening, in the local dialect. In so far as the knowledge of Sanskrit language is concerned, he considered that only the Pracharya (principal) of the Post Graduate Sanskrit College of the entire district could match his proficiency in the language. We can take his boast with a pinch of salt as intellectuals are after all arrogant. Adamant as he was, it was nothing short of a blasphemous declaration, against the established religious practices and traditions. His own nephews, led by Sunder Singh, revolted against him and he had to change his mind; to the relief of everybody, including the family priest. The other peculiar characteristic of his personality was chess for which he was known in the entire police department. After retirement, he would walk miles to neighbouring villages to play chess. At times he was so engrossed in the game that he forgot time and search parties had to be dispatched in the night to locate him. He had yet another peculiar trait in his professional personality, he possessed a compulsiveness to harbour the absconding freedom fighters within the police station. His idea was to enable them to hide from the eyes of the law- this was definitely an offence under the existing British draconian law. Thus, he invariably got suspended for dereliction of duty. He was however fortunate enough, to get exonerated by the courts of law for lack of evidence and always got reinstated. After all who would depose against a Station House Office? Thus, a young girl, a student of MA, final in literature in Allahabad University, got married to Satya Pratap Singh; a resident of village Arki in Banda district (now Chitrakoot). It is not known as to how the village Arki got its name, but there is definitely a place called Arki in Himachal Pradesh. This in local dialect means a place of serenity and happiness. Village Arki was in reality a god-forsaken place in those days. It could be accessed only by crossing the mighty river Yamuna at a place called Rajapur and another river called Paiswini at Arki. It was impossible even to think of visiting the village during the monsoon season. As the village was located approximately ten kilometers from the road head, the newlywed girl had the royal privilege of negotiating the distance in a palanquin. Contrary to their past experiences the palanquin bearers were delighted to transport such a feather weight occupant without any physical strain. It was really a unique experience for the bride because she had only seen the villages from a distance as her father had a car for intercity movements if considered absolutely necessary. The new bride was welcomed with an open heart in her new abode. She was really a centre of attraction and admiration being a university girl. The thumb impressionist lady relatives considered themselves heavily empowered finding her amongst them and conferred the title of Sahebain (the lady officer) by which she is still addressed and remembered even often her sad demise in July 2013. She forgot totally the slaughter of her own dreams and aspirations, in such a genuinely cordial and friendly environment. There was no question of a honeymoon since her husband was transferred to the Infantry School (now called College of Combat) within a few days of marriage to undergo commando training. It is the toughest course of the Indian army, second only to the Rangers course of the US Army. Just visualise a doctor and an ambulance accompanying the trainees all along the entire duration of the course. Ten per cent of the casualties in the training are treated as battle casualties in a war.

Her ordeal was far from over. Just after the husband returned from the course, her yet worse was to come. For the mandatory rituals her husband was transferred to a non-family station in a forward brigade in Jammu & Kashmir. Here enemy troops faced each other at some places, from hand shaking distance. Ironically, the Pakistanis used to call the Indian brigade a Chutney brigade. To counter their psychological mischief, Indians named their brigade 'Shakti-Vijay' brigade. The Indian army proved beyond doubt in the show of strength in 1965 and 1971 by, humiliating their boastful adversaries.

Since the bride was on a family way and no medical facilities worth any mention existed in the village she was shifted to Allahabad where her father was posted as City Magistrate. The news of child birth to reached his father after a considerable time since like Indian soldiers, even letters had to negotiate the high peaks of the Pir Panchal mountain range in J&K. In those days, phones were a great luxury and simply not available and mobile phones had not yet been invented.

There was no way to celebrate the auspicious occasion in an operational brigade. Therefore, a quiz competition, was arranged, involving the officers of the brigade. which was posted in high, snow covered peaks (it was telephonically managed dysfunctional reality show besides being good past-time which was the only intellectually engaging activity.

Consensus emerged in favour of the 'SARAL, the name for the new born. Linguistically speaking, there can be no simple word in the vocabulary of any modern language the name was contrary to the existing practice of naming a child with imaginative fancy and even unpronounceable names. The name given to the child was forwarded to Army Headquarters for entry in official documents to entitle the child the legal right of inheritance and other attendant entitlements. The Army Headquarters publishes these joyful events in a document officially called 'Returns' in military parlance. We really fail to understand the sad humour of the person who coined this word. The discharge booklet issued by the Army to Sharad's father still carries the name 'Saral, contrary to the name Sharad as known today. The grandfather of Sharad passed away in Sep. 1967. The death of the family patriarch seriously damages the fabric of unity in a family and Singh's family was no exception. Although he had brought financial status of the family on even keel by sheer dent of self-inflicted financial injury to his own interests but everyone simply forgot his contribution. All the other brothers were acting in their own self interest. The bride who was given a heart-warming welcome only a few months back was no longer a welcome in the village and she had to stay with her father at Allahabad. In a way, she became a refugee in her own house. During the intervening period, Singh was blessed with a daughter but the situation took a bad turn when he was released from the army. Uncertain of his future, he again resumed his academic interests and obtained a post graduate degree from the University of Sagar as a private candidate. Simultaneously, he also qualified in the Civil Services Examination in 1969 and was awaiting his posting order in his new career. Devoid of any savings, his wife had to stay in her parent's village because her own father had retired from service. It must have been very embarrassing socially that his newly married daughter was not living with her husband. It was equally strange that her husband's brothers who were by now well established in their gainful careers, had no sympathy towards Singh, although directly or indirectly they had benefited from his misplaced idealism As there were no facilities of healthcare in her parent's village, she shifted again to separated Officer's flats at Hasting Road near Allahabad High Court along with her two small kids. The only company she had was the mazar of a Pir baba located across the flats. This was the only source of strength for her.

An incident needs mention here as it has direct bearing on the change of the boy's name from Saral to Sharad. When Saral's father was preparing for UPSC interview' elder brother Dr M.P. Singh, who was an associate professor in Delhi University advised him to update his understanding of the epic Ramayana written by Tulsi Das a native of Rajapur, few miles away from their ancestral village. The advice was however never heeded. To his utter surprise, the first question the presiding officer of the UPSC Board posed was on the Ramayana itself. Singh had no clues to the answer but he suddenly remembered how his father used to recite the verses from Valmiki Ramayana to his illiterate mother and translate the same in Hindi. The presiding officer was highly impressed by his shallow knowledge and shifted to other subjects, like the security situation in the country and economics etc. Highly relieved Singh became a voracious reader of Ram Charit Manas and continues to do so even today. We would like to emphasise that the epic is less of a religious scripture and more of a social treatise and store house of ethical values.

In due course the young couple shifted to Bombay on receipt of the appointment letter. It was a great relief from the trials, tribulations and sufferings of his initial three years of married life.

Five decades back, in any cultured Hindu family it was taboo to give even an innocent glance or smile to a newly wed wife, any such act easily became a hot topic of gossip amongst the youth of the village. The transfer to a new place gave them ample moments to express their feelings to each other. Before we come to the crux of the matter there are compelling reasons to narrate an incident as penned down by the epic poet Tulsi Das. When the lord Rama was constructing the bridge (Setu bund) to cross over to Lanka; the monkey force used to write 'Ram' on the stones and throw them into the sea. Surprisingly these stones, instead of sinking in the sea bed floated on the surface. Lord Ram was flabbergasted by this strange phenomenon and out of sheer curiosity, picked up a stone and threw it into the sea. To his utter surprise the stone immediately sank in the sea. He asked the reasons thereof to his most wise counseller Hanuman, who enlightened Ram that since the name Ram was not written on the stone it sank immediately. Thus, a name has tremendous significance.

The posting in Bombay gave an excellent opportunity to the parents to express their views without any inhibitions. Mithlesh, the mother, found that the name 'Saral' conveyed an identity of being a simpleton and suggested a change. They did find an answer together in a couplet where epic poet

Tulsidas describes the Sharad ritu after the monsoon is over. It reads:

भूमि जीव संकुल रहे। गये शरद ऋतु आय।
सद्गुरु मिले जाहि जिम। संशय भ्रम समुदाय

Loosely translated this means that in autumn season, pure nature is at its splendid best with a vast and clear sky. The season is akin to an enlightened teacher where there is no room for any illusion or ambiguity. A name thus constantly motivates one to live up to the intrinsic meaning of the name given to one. We feel that there is everything in the name if one really understands what it connotes. Saral thus became Sharad, a new identity tag given by the parents where there was really no space for any illusion or ambiguity.

# Chapter II

# The Uninvited Miseries

Some wise man has said that little knowledge is a dangerous thing. This saying fits completely in the attitude of Sharad's father whom we shall now refer to as SP, was the manner by which he was addressed by his army colleagues and also in the civil service. He had heard from one of his genuinely wise friends that any wealth has three stages. First, if the riches are there, these should be enjoyed. Secondly, if there is any balance left it should be spent on charity. Thirdly, if the wealth does not pass through these two stages it gets destroyed automatically. Without understanding the import of the Sanskrit maxim as narrated above, he developed disproportional attitude to charity, the consequence of which proved to be too detrimental for the well-being of his own family.

The selection of SP into the civil services brought immense joy and happiness to the family. However, some members thought that the Manipur Civil Service, the cadre which he was allotted would not be of any help to the well being of the family as he was likely to be away in the north-east. With the help of a close acquaintance in the Union Ministry, an influential member of the family, got his allotment to the service changed to the Customs and Excise Department in the Finance Ministry. Their main intention however, was, that since the

Customs was a very lucrative service where money could be made incorrupted, SP would be very pliable to be exploited financially. He was thus perforce compelled to join Bombay Customs as an Appraising Officer in Feb. 1971.

Though he was earning a handsome salary in the army, he was however simultaneously burning it illogically on his relations who had formed a coterie around him solely to enjoy his hard earned money. Many may not believe this but he had no savings even to purchase a ticket to join his new place of posting. It was a friend of his school days who voluntarily came forward and arranged the financial resources to embark upon his new career.

*Dr Sharad Chauhan IPS*
*Inspector General of Police*

*With Sapna his Sister who is*
*co-author of the Book*

Army officers by temperament are very conscious of their rank and take great pride in their status in the society. The Custons deptartment was located in a building, ironically called the New Custom House which was in fact a converted military Hospital in the First World War. It wore not only a ghostly look, but was said to be frequented by ghosts in the night. The working conditions were appalling. There were no cabins for the gazetted officers and functionaries of the department had their desks in the open halls where all officers from Group A down to the sepoy level worked in perfect harmony. The Right to equality was best exhibited here. There was nothing opaque around you and visitors could easily see not only the brandy but also the quantity of the cigarettes you smoked while on the job. The concept of constructing cabins for the Gazetted Officer crept in only when few young girls too started joining the class one service after competing in the Civil Service examination. It was an unavoidable necessity to save the poor girls from curious ogling of the onlookers.

With half the salary which SP was earning in the army, he had now three mouths to feed. As there was hardly any residential accommodation for the officers, the bulk of the salary was used for paying the rent of a rented accommodation. Apparently such financial constraints had a telling effect on the health of the members of the family. But it was SP who became the first victim of the misery which was stalking closely. He got totally incapacitated and was unable to even stand or walk. He was totally bedridden for a period of four months by a disease called disc Syndrome in the medical parlance.

This peculiar disease was unheard of north of Vindhya Mountain ranges and in Bombay it was called the bus conductors disease because the poor chaps are constantly subjected to sudden jerks in performance of their strenuous job. Gradually even people from upper strata of the society started falling victim to this crippling disability and to save themselves from the ignominy of being bracketed with the bus conductors, a rumour was spread that the disease was caused by sedentary life style. This is the most dreaded disease in the United States because it takes away millions of work hours which are very detrimental to the economic health of the nation. Whatever may be the truth, nobody knows for sure as to why it happens and there is no definite treatment except complete bed rest, strong doses of pain killers and physiotherapy. Currently, with the advancement of the technology, interventional therapy is now being used successfully. In early seventies there was no MR1 or CAT scan and the only diagnostic aid available was a Mylogram a painful procedure for injecting a **** repeated x-ray we take to identify the specific area needing surgical intervention.

Since SP had joined the service only a few months back he had hardly thirty days leave entitlements to his credit. The rest leave was allowed with half pay and bulk of it without pay. There was hardly any money even to pay the doctor's visiting fee. It was really a very benevolent gesture on part of Dr B.V. Bawadekar an orthopedic surgeon of great repute of the K E M Hospital who visited the patient, driving in his own car miles away, without charging any fees. The financial hardship had a very telling and detrimental effect on the health of his wife also who notwithstanding her fragile frame, an infant of two years of age on the lap and a school bag on her shoulders had to walk kilometers to save a few coins for emergency.

Pleasures and pains are inevitable in life but what was more painful was the stony silence and indifference of certain members of the family who had resources to bail out his brother who had spent everything, whatever he had earned to help others. Ultimately, it was Mata Bux Singh a retired civil servant who sent it a princely amount of Rs 4000 to his daughter to tide over the acute financial crises. This was a princely amount four decades ago. There is no intention to put these facts in public domain except to highlight the fact that people have very false and funny notion that Customs Officers are like the Sultan of Brunei island who sleeps on wads of currency notes. We are definitely not pointing any accusing finger on any one for their poor perception of the realities of the Custom Service. Sharad for none of his faults was baptized in these trying circumstances.

Life after sometime, started changing for the better as army seniority was added to the Civil Service, and correspondingly salary was also enhanced. Meanwhile his provident fund and gratuity from the army service was also released and life became bearable. Meanwhile, the physical disability of SP also improved and he was able to join his job. He had to wear, however, a cumbersome and heavy sacro-lumbar steel belt to keep the back in an upright position. It may be of interest to know that in the early seventies, these orthopedic belts were not manufactured in any organised industrial sector in Bombay and a private middle class entrepreneur in Thane district of Maharashtra state was the sole manufacturer. He used to visit hospitals and nursing homes in an around Bombay to take measurements to manufacture the product. Although it was made of steel and was heavy, yet it was a great relief to suffering patients.

Miseries never have any soft corner for a targeted individual and visit him on and off like weather. The one thing very definite about the disc syndrome is that it is very adamant in nature and keeps on visiting the helpless patient at the time of its own choosing. However, since it is not life threatening, one can always rise to fight it again and again. The golden rule to ward it off is to follow the principle that one should not be timid at the same time do not be reckless as well.

The anxiety, uncertainty, depression and unimaginable financial hardships had a very damaging impact on the mother of Sharad and she was reduced to a bundle of thirty four kgs in a span of four months and collapsed in the kitchen one day while cooking. Thus, yet another misery had struck again within a short period.

Virtually unknown to the city, a family doctor was consulted for guidance. The family physician, Dr Bhal S. Patil was a very interesting personality. While even in his clinic, he used to write Marathi novels whenever there were no patients around. It was learnt much later that the Marathi novels authored by him were prescribed for regular study of Marathi literature in the post graduate courses of Bombay University.

He was not only a literary figure but also a socio-political activist and thus commanded a lot of respect not only in society, but also in the medical fraternity. He had yet another peculiar characteristic. Although he had his clinic on the ground floor of his bungalow, he resided on the first floor. He had given liberty to his clients to visit him at his residence beyond working hours of the clinic even at odd hours only to those patients who had literary inclinations. Needless to say, he never charged any consultation fee for such visits at his residential apartment. On the contrary, Nalini Bhal Paul, his gracious wife, sent back the patient smiling with a generous gift of fresh vegetables from her kitchen garden. SP was one of the few patients who were extended this facility, the always addressed as KAVIRAJ. It appears that he had joined the medical profession by default.

We have no clue as to the doctor immediately referred the case to one Dr K.K. Datey, an eminent cardiologist of international repute who besides being Padma Bhushan awardees was also the honorary physician to the President of India. It was no easy job to get an appointment with him, since he did not see more than four patients in a day and there was a long waiting list. He was also head of the Cardiology dept. of the Bombay Hospital; one of the most famous hospitals, in India in those days. His consultation fees were also abnormally high by any standards of those days. Needless, to say, he was assisted by a battery of young and brilliant doctors, whom he picked up personally from the medical colleges itself. But for Dr Bhal Patil nothing was impossible and he got an appointment for the same day.

Without any pathological or clinical tests, he diagnosed the disease and said that she was suffering from Colitis. There was only one follow-up visit for further check-up and there after the patient never visited any doctor for the next thirty years. During the second visit he did not charge any remuneration for the consultation fee when he learnt that his patient was a student of Allahabad University, his own alma mater. He himself was a graduate of the said university, before he switched over to medical studies for his career in the medicine profession.

The only ray of hope in those trying circumstances was the proprietor of the Deen Bandhu General Stores, a grocery shop owned by a Gujarati gentleman on Andheri-Versova road who kept supplying groceries for months together in spite of non-payment of the dues. Also the St Xavier High School which charged only five rupees fee per month for a quality education which we cannot dream of today. Sharad's parents always remember the two with a great sense of gratitude.

We cannot say with any certainty as to what was agitating the mind of the small child as Sharad was hardly four years old at that time but it must not have been a very pleasant experience to see his parents running from pillar to post from one doctor to another. A child may not speak much but such an environment deeply influences his mind. As we know, the human mind is a super computer where nothing can be deleted and therefore it appears that the idea of becoming a doctor must have taken a deep root in his subconscious mind during his early years of life itself. After all a child starts writing the script of his destiny from the mother's womb itself.

# Chapter III

# Adventure Unprecedented

Of late, there is a strong debate amongst the intellectuals with regard to the prospects and repercussions of developing genetically modified crops. Our statement may appear to be preposterous but there have been attempts to raise a genetically modified human race too in our history.

During the Second World War, after the landing in Normandy in France, the allied forces while advancing in Germany, found a strange camp which was inhabited by young but pregnant ladies. Surprisingly there was no male around in the entire vast habitat. Hitler, had, besides other notorious detention camps, created 'love camps' where young ladies were compelled to live as husband and wife with the gallantry award winners of the German Army. Once the ladies conceived the soldiers were despatched again to the war front for their duties. In fact, Hitler wanted to create an altogether superior Aryan race with such perverse experiments. Now we cannot blame anyone from holding the view that the brute had no delicate feelings for human emotions.

We have play school for children and when they attain the age of three years they are pushed into these schools. You may witness the scenario yourself by visiting these schools. The child is no more a mischievous kid but sober, not flamboyant anymore but a disciplined person. So much so, that the identity of the child has shrunk to an identity tag which is hung proudly around his neck. What we want to emphasise is that society is denying the child his precious childhood and pushing the infant to adulthood by skipping the natural stages of the development of the child. It may not be something like genetic modification but the rat race is no less dangerous. A heavy load of books and study material, tuition classes and coaching classes for the child are in fact manifestations of this competitive phenomenon and at best our own blatant efforts to camouflage our own incompetency and failures because in doing so our sole intention is to escape the insecurities of our own future life.

The city of Bombay offers multiple choices of well-established schools both English medium as well as being run in other Indian languages medium. Hindi is given equal importance and the child develops the competence and skill to think and communicate in multiple languages. Most of the English medium schools in the city are Christian schools and have some linkage with the Vatican in Italy for their financial support. Principals of these schools are identified popularly by their designation as Father or 'Reverend Father'. Their appointments and transfers are also controlled by the church they belong to and thus they have sufficient freedom to discharge their responsibilities in a just and fair manner for each and every child admitted in the school. External influences like recommendations, donations or political and bureaucratic influences to get admissions hardly works here. There was a well-known story about a very famous actor in the film industry. Since the actor was too busy in a film shoot, he sent his wife to get his son admitted to a very famous Jesuist school. The admission was refused only on the ground that there is no place for the child in his school when his father had no time to be with his son on such an eventful day.

Sharad got admission in St Xavier High School located at Ville Parle, a suburb in north Bombay. It was a very renowned school with vast play grounds and a magnificent old church of Anglo-gothic style of architecture located within the school premises. The faculty was a dedicated band of teachers, so essential for the unhampered growth of a child's mind. As the very first day of the admission, the Rev Father addressed the gathering of the parents and told them to firstly 'grow with the child' and secondly `never send the child for private tuitions' and promised the gathering that if the child was found wanting in any subject the school would make arrangements for them to be on par with other fellow students. The Principal of the school was of the definite view that the practice of private tuition curbs the intellectual curiosity of the child and makes him unnecessarily dependent on extraneous help.

The first progress report card of the child was very demoralising for the mother of Sharad. The remark was very short and simple and read "very talkative. May God bless him." The mother thought that there was some problem with the child and therefore the teacher was invoking mercy of the God. Her fears were however allayed when her husband interpreted the observation to the effect that only an intelligent child of his age could engage himself in talk and the teacher was simply giving her blessings to the child. The evidence of teacher's blessing was evident when a simple table of mathematical addition was given to him as homework. It can best be explained only by reconstructing his effort in the shape of a table. As against the simple method of learning in the school which is shown as exhibit 'A' he solved the sum in his own style as shown in the exhibit 'B'. While solving sums of simple addition, a child is taught to proceed to from right to left (as shown in exhibit A) but his curiosity new no bounds and he solved the sum by going from left to right (as shown in exhibit B) and the answer was too bizarre to go unnoticed.

Exhibit B (unconventional method)

| | | | |
|---|---|---|---|
| | 1 | 2 | 3 |
| + | 4 | 5 | 6 |
| + | 7 | 8 | 9 |
| 1 | 3 | 6 | 7 |

Exhibit A (conventional method)

| | | | |
|---|---|---|---|
| | 1 | 2 | 3 |
| + | 4 | 5 | 6 |
| + | 7 | 8 | 9 |
| 2 | 6 | 1 | 9 |

We are told by his mother that she gave him a hard slap. We however refuse to believe her, since she was incapable of displaying her displeasure in such an unpleasant manner. Intellectuals think out of the box and have proclivity not to tread on a beaten track. In any case the coming events had begun casting their shadow as the intellectual misadventure of the child clearly conveys to us.

The opening para of our introduction to this chapter most definitely have aroused many questions in the readers but we, it was not out of context. The incident which will follow now will explain how irrational ambitions can create very awkward situations. It was a hot and humid day of May in 1978. The scenario of this type are seldom witnessed in his life time. There was a huge gathering of children, over a thousand, of different age groups varying from ten to fifteen years of age, jostling around. Some of them were accompanied by their parents. Since Bombay Customs had inadequate space to accommodate such a large crowd, they had temporarily requisitioned the venue from the Indian Naval Authority in Ballard Peer and declared it a Custom Area to carry out Customs and Immigration formalities for the children who were going to undertake a voyage to South East Asian Countries by sea route.

Shri Z B Nagarkar, the then Asstt Commissioner of Customs, was supervising the entire procedure. He suddenly saw a boy of hardly ten years of age approaching the immigration official with a rare confidence along with his travel documents all by himself. Seeing such a small child not accompanied by his parents or a guardian, he enquired from one of the custom officer as to who this boy was. Nagarkar was informed that he was the son of an officer from their own fraternity. He was aghast with the surprise, about the callous attitude of his brother officer who left his child alone and got

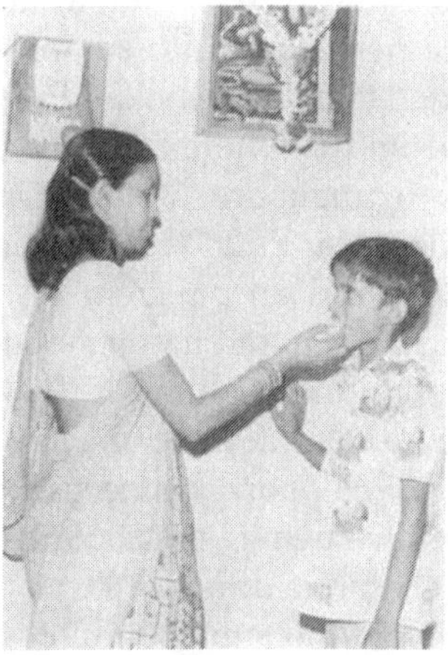

*Sweet Welcome by the Mother after returning from Solo Cruise to South Asian Countries in May 1978. In Steamship Noorjahan*

*After Return of South East Asia Solo Tour at the Age of Ten Years*

him located in the crowd. He rebuked the father of the child in disgust for sending such a small boy, all alone in such a long voyage to foreign lands. The father with due courtesy, informed Nagarkar that lions do not move in herds. His answer betrayed the confidence. Nagarkar, was however more pragmatic, and directed the custom officer to locate some responsible family who could be designated as guardians for the child. Resourceful as the custom officers are, he located a Sindhi gentleman who was accompanying his three daughters. In fact, the person who was identified as a potential guardian had lost his wife in the recent past and was taking his children just for a change to divert their mind. He was extremely gentleman and accepted the added responsibility very gladly. The child who was proceeding alone on the long voyage was none other than Sharad.

The background to this arrangement of foreign visits for the kids is equally amusing. The Steamship Noor Jehan was a passenger liner in the business of ferrying passengers from Indian shores to East Asian Countries and was shortly scheduled for decommissioning. It was soon to be sent to ship-yard for ship breaking. Before being turned into scrap, the management of the company decided to do some philanthropic work. They invited applications from the whole of India and selected 1000 childrens free visits to Singapore, Malaysia and Ceylon. The total cost for each student was Rs 2000 and parents had the option to accompany the child on payment of the requisite expenses. Since the parents of Sharad had no money they decided to send the child all alone by himself. It was indeed an unprecedented adventure to undertake which was thrust upon the child. Leave alone telephone connection, in the early seventies, it was a big achievement if one could get a milk card to purchase the government dairy milk at the subsidised rate. Letters were the only tools to communicate, to inform or misinform, to guide or misguide or to love or hate someone. Apparently by the time the letter reached an addressee, and cognisance thereof could be taken, valuable time was lost and any course correction was simply not feasible.

The news of the departure of Sharad, all alone by himself to distant shore, thus reached the grandfather of Sharad late as he had settled in a village after his retirement from the government service. He was at his wits end and did not really know as to how to react to the foolish decision of his son-in-law. Realising the sensitivity of his relations he kept cool but did convey his displeasure in no uncertain terms. However, there were numerous relations who had no qualms in condemning such a risky decision.

In the opening para of this chapter we started in a philosophical note as to how the childhood of an infant is being snatched just to make him an adult prematurely by the parents in pursuance of their own agenda. We really cannot blame the parents for such disoriented thinking. Idealism which acted as an adhesive to give harmony and cohesiveness to the institution of the family has been badly eroded and is now replaced by selfish economic interests. More than the economic security of the child parents are now paranoid and haunted by their own insecurity. The real answer to their irrational thinking and behaviour is carefully concealed in their own infirmities be these either physical or mental. There was sufficient evidence to conclude that father of Sharad was passing through the worst phase of uncertainty and anxiety owing to poor physical health of his own and also of his wife.

We have to accept the fact that currently the institution of the family is under great stress. The reasons are obvious to all of us. The greed to nurture our economic interests by fair or foul methods is the root cause of unethical behaviour. It is not that our ancestors could not foresee such anomaly to raise its ugly head in our behaviour. There is a proverb in eastern Uttar Pradesh "*hamari hoi humkhai, tumhari hoi hum khai, hamar tumhar koi bata thodi hai*" (If it belongs to us we eat and if it belongs to you we eat. After all we are one). It is fair enough if we safeguard our own economic interests; but the emphasis in our thinking, is to grab someone else legitimate economic assets. This sets in motion conflict amongst the stakeholders of the institution and fuels economic insecurity. The victim of this degrading phenomenon is the innocent child who has to skip the natural phases of growth to become an adult prematurely wisdom dawned on Sharad's parents but it was too late, as Noor Jehan had left the Indian shores. There was no way to retrace the steps except to pray for his safe return from the adventurous journey. All said and done, the voyage had tremendous influence on the mind of the young boy. The vast infinite blue sky above, the constant chatting of sea waves of the Arabian Sea, Bay of Bengal and the Pacific, the silvery shining beaches in the foreign lands added vision to his delicate emotions and thinking. A letter he wrote to his parents on the paper napkin of the dining table clearly indicated that he had by now a mind of his own. It may seem strange but none the less true that even foolishness arising out of noble intentions can bring a positive result in the personality of a child.

**(We are trying our best to locate this letter from the belongings of the late mother of Sharad. There must be something extra ordinary in its contents otherwise she must not have it as most cherished treasure.)**

Emotional torture however gave way to the cheerful smile on the faces of his parents when after 15 days, the steamship Noor Jehan arrived in Bombay. The family was there to extend a rousing welcome to the child at the Ballard Pier Naval Jetty. All eyes were glued to the gangway (a ladder lowered for the passengers to alight) and there came out the hero of the solo journey, all cheerful and confident. Even the English must have not felt that much pride and joy when the legendary British Admiral Nelson had returned to England after defeating the French Navy in the battle of Trafalgar. The semaphore flags hoisted on board the ship while entering the harbour read "England expects everyman to do his duty". To his parent Sharad had done his duty by respecting the desires of his parents to undertake such an adventurous journey willingly and smilingly, while he was just in double digits of his age.

## Chapter IV

# The Mother - A Role Model

The disc syndrome is a peculiar disability and it always remains loyal to the person to whom it visits and establishes a lifelong agonising relationship. It goes away of its own free will however, returns at the time of its own choosing. The diagnosis of the disc syndrome as coined by the physician is not easily understood. It usually occurs in the low back region of the vertebra owing to the decay of the soft jelly like tissue called disc between the two vertebras and seriously affects the mobility of the patient and causes unbearable radiating pain right up to the toes as the disc protrudes and exerts its pressure on the spinal cord. The patient is totally incapacitated and suffers from agonising pain, only heavy doses of pain killers and cortisone injections bring relief to the patient. Surgical intervention is considered only as a last resort. Acupuncture, a Chinese line of treatment, where silver needles are inserted in numerous nerves also gives relief but does not grant complete cure. However, there was only one, Dr Billiporia who had specialised this line of treatment in whole of Bombay city. Ayurvedic doctors too recommended certain specially manufactured oils besides certain manipulative exercises. One doctor named Dr Mathew George from Ernakulum city in Kerala state invented yet another line of treatment called Magnetic Therapy where affected parts are exposed to electro-magnetic impulses.

Even quacks have a field day in their business as they advocate if a child whose legs appear first at the time of birth gives a kick on the back of the patient he is completely cured. Since the patient was a permanent client of the syndrome out of sheer helplessness he tried all the above stated therapies but of no avail. However, after about over two decades of physical suffering, he was operated successfully by Dr Rajesh Navalkar, an orthopedic surgeon of the Jaslok Hospital in Bombay in 1997.

As the name of the Jaslok Hospital has crept in, there is a very interesting incident related with it which needs mention. Just to demonstrate there are persons/ institutes of repute who become grateful to you for life even for your small kind gestures, Jaslok Hospital in South Bombay was coming up in early seventies and they had imported a GAMA camera, a

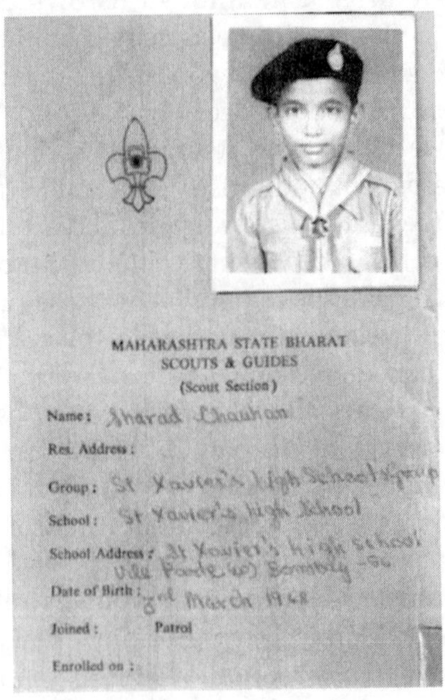


*As Cadet of Maharashtra State Scouts and Guides*

diagnostic equipment for cancer patients from France. It was a very costly equipment but they had no money to pay the customs duty which amounted to over one crore rupees. The trust of the hospital applied for the waiver of customs duties to the Govt. of India, but it was time consuming and the equipment could not be kept un-cleared because if it was not stored at eight degree centigrade temperature, it would become non-functional and the defect could only be rectified by French engineers at a colossal cost. The Director of the Hospital approached the customs for a way out. The superior officer of Sharad's father was asked if he could pass the equipment without payment of duty as adhoc examination may or may not be granted to the hospital but was told in uncertain terms that there was every possibility of his suspension if the omission was detected before the receipt of the waiver of custom duty. Singh preferred the option of dereliction of duty and impending suspension for larger interests of the suffering patients and cleared the equipment free of duty. The then Director of the hospital Dr Shanti Lal Mehta personally expressed his gratitude to Sharad's father and ordered his Director of the Administration one Dr Suresh Karnik to make a permanent note that no fee or medical expenses be charged from Singh throughout his life time. Dr Karnik was also not an ordinary doctor. He was the only doctor holding a PhD degree on nuclear medicine in whole of Asia. He was specially requested to join the Jaslok Hospital and came back from the United States where he was engaged in further research. He did come back and was offered a salary equivalent to that of the Director of the hospital. The Trustees of the Hospital honoured their commitment given to the father of Sharad about two and a half decade earlier and refunded the entire amount of expenses of surgery and hospitalisation. Indeed gratefulness is the biggest virtue which we can exhibit to our fellow citizens.

It was in such a gloomy and uncertain future that the mother of Sharad decided to take a plunge and meet the challenges head on as she was unable to accept the cruel dictates of the destiny any more. Only Pune University allowed women to pursue studies as an external student. The University also offered the option of completing two-year post graduation course in a year itself if a student had confidence on her capabilities. Since time factor was at a premium she decided to complete her post-graduation in an academic year itself. Apparently this facility was available only to ladies so that housewives could be encouraged to enhance their academic qualifications. It was a very kind gesture on the part of the Pune University and therefore it is rightly called the Cultural Capital of Maharashtra.

Nothing was ensure to fulfil such a bold commitment. In a one room tenement, small children used to be pushed away in the balcony so that they did not disturb her studies. When intentions are noble and efforts are sincere even God has no choice but to willingly fulfil one's dreams. Her husband's friend, an army doctor, who was posted at the Artificial Limb Centre Pune, proceeded on two months leave, to ensure that his army accommodation was at her disposal during the course of her examination. This solved the problem of not only boarding and lodging but also ensured the safety of the kids as the flat was a part of the army officer's enclave in the cantonment area. Her brother-in-law Major Awadhesh (husband's younger brother) who was posted in Siachin glacier took two months leave to accompany her to ensure that everything proceeded smoothly in an unknown city. The army doctor referred to was Sushil Kumar Jain from Kanpur in UP who had done his Master of Surgery from the King George Medical College Lucknow and MPhil from Birmingham University in UK to inventing artificial limbs. He later rose to the rank of Major General in the Army Medical Corps after commanding the Artificial Limb Centre. He had a very strange take on the medical profession. He firmly believed that ninety per cent illness did not require any treatment as the human body was capable of taking care of itself. The next five per cent could be cured by subjecting the body to certain required discipline and it was only a five per cent of patients who required any medical/ surgical intervention. No wonder in his initial career in the army as a young captain he was usually found in the weapon firing range with his camera than available in his clinic called medical inspection room (MI Room). Fortunately, he has modified his thinking radically later and has become a full-fledged doctor.

The results of the MA examination were very inspiring. In spite of being an external student, she had obtained a very high second division and surprisingly her marks in linguistics and literary criticism were much higher than those of the regular students. The Faculty of Hindi Literature in the University was highly impressed with her performance and she was suo motu offered assistane to carry out the doctoral research. Dr Maurya, the Head of the Hindi Dept., was designated her guide for research and the subject for thesis allotted to her was "Hindi mein deshaj shabd" (The colloquial words of Hindi dialect in Hindi Literature). Unfortunately, Dr Maurya suffered a stroke and was incapacitated. He could not fulfil his assignment and thus the effort to do the research in Pune University was abandoned half way. It is said that the God helps those who help themselves. The news of abrupt discontinuation of her doctoral effort came to the notice of the Hindi Dept of Bombay University. In due course, the university therefore offered her to research in the field of literary criticism. The subject allotted to her for research was "The romantic criticism in Hindi Literature." It was naturally a very new concept and the thought of any substantial research on the subject essentially borrowed much from the concept of romantic criticism in the English literature. The subject was to her liking and temperament and therefore she gladly accepted the offer. She completed her thesis in a record time of two years and obtained the prefix of Doctor to her name in the year 1982. Her research has since been published by reputed publishers at Kanpur (UP) although they were never approached with any such offer of request. It was indeed a rare display of grit, determination and diligence in the face of numerous challenges. Even Prof Ram Joshi, the then Vice Chancellor of Bombay University was so pleased with her work that he offered her job of lecturer in the University. The offer was politely declined although the same could have ensured much needed relief to the financial constraint the family was then facing. She considered bringing up children more important than bringing a pay packet home.

It was a great sacrifice not only on the part of the mother but also on the part of the two small children as well who used to persistently request in their feeble voice to be allowed to come in the room from the balcony of the flat where they were driven out by her to concentrate on her studies. The children were unable to understand the reasons why they were subjected to such ill treatment but they did realise something great was shaping and therefore suffered in silence with unusual dignity.

The Mother of Sharad was a vorocious reader and always kept abreast with the latest thinking on education and personality development. When the question of joining NCC or Bharat Scouts and Guides came up before her to make a choice, she preferred the later as it had more extracurricular activity in comparisons to the NCC. She had timely gathered useful inputs on the choices offered a head of line. To her the Boys scouts and girls guides appealed more not because of its older origin. It had been started in 1907 when a retired army General, Lord Baden Powell ls-tnt- in England. This organisation laid emphasis on emotional, social and spiritual potential to make an individual a responsible citizen in a local national and international community. A rare photograph of Sharad in an uniform of Bharat Scouts & Guide is exhibited opposite.

By sacrificing her own comforts and by her constant effort to empower her personality she became a role model for her children. It was a great stimuli in helping her children to develop their own personality and equip themselves to face the challenges of life successfully.

# Chapter V

# In Search of a Spring Board

The Father of Sharad was transferred to Delhi in March 1983 on his promotion and posted in the Directorate of Revenue Intelligence. Since Sharad was yet to clear his matric examination, the anxiety of getting a right type of school in the new location occupied most of his mind.

School admission is the most important event in the life in a child of since the right school acts as an ideal spring board for ultimate success. To add to the confusion, there are numerous categories of schools, like, government schools, private schools, aided and non-aided schools. Now even yet another category of school namely, 'International schools' have mushroomed in the field of education. To select the right type of school and get admission is really a nightmare for parents. Goverment schools owing to their poor infrastructure and unsatisfactory teacher-student ratio appear to be the least preferred, although such prejudice appears to be unreasonable as their performance in the respective Examination Boards is very inspiring. Public schools, on the contrary, are definitely beyond the reach of the middle class income group, owing to their exorbitant fees and therefore are kept aside of the admission plan. The choice therefore narrowed down to a very few schools. As the number of parents seeking admissions to these schools is very large to succeed in getting admission to

*On an Education Tour to Harmandier Saheb (Golden Temple) Amritsar at Twelve Years of Age.*

these schools is no less effort than winning a medal in an Olympic game.

In such a cut throat competitive scenario, political clout or bureaucratic pressures was the only possible remedy available whereas the father of Sharad had none. Of course, the parents had anticipated the problem and had become life members of Bhartiya Vidya Bhawan society in Bombay. The society was also running Bhartiya Vidya Bhavan School on Kasturba Gandhi Marg in Delhi, and the fond hope that such membership will come handy in getting the admission. It may be relevant to state that the Vidya Bhawan Trust has a vast education Complex in Andheri (West), a north suburb of Bombay, where they have educational institutes providing education right from the kindergarten level up to post-doctoral level even in the field on engineering and management studies. As an abundant precaution, a recommendatory letter was also obtained from the General Secretary of the trust to ensure smooth success in getting the admission.

The concept of elite schools is something we have inherited as a legacy. The old Gurukuls which were the centres for imparting education were tilted in favour of the ruling elite and were not at all fair or inclusive. Guru Dronacharya admitted only the royal Kshatriya siblings in the Gurukul and is therefore rightly called the pioneer of the public schools in modern day concept of the public schools. Eklavya, a bright student but from a lowly caste, was refused admission in the Gurukul only on this account. The great preacher-soldier Parashuram never admitted a child of the Kshatriya clan and Karan, the epic hero of the Mahabharata war, succeeded in getting admission in his gurukul only by cleverly concealing his caste. The trend continues to persist even today, of course, in disguised forms. Right to education can never achieve its cherished goals if the disparity in infrastructural layout and standards of education are not brought on par within the various types of the schools which exist all across India. The government is wide awake to this abnormal gap and has rightly passed a legislation making it mandatory to aided public schools to admit thirty per cent of their students from the economically weaker sections of the society.

With the recommendatory letter in his pocket, for the school admission, the father of Sharad thought that the job was done. Little did he realise the folly of his judgment and deficiency of practical wisdom to conclude that way. The mad scramble for admissions to these schools can be understood against this background only. Making no headway, father of Sharad remembered a colleague in Bombay who used to boast to his friends that he was educated in Delhi-Canada School in Delhi. Assuming it to be a school run by the Canadian Embassy which must be having a very high standard of teaching he was requested if he could help in securing the admission in that school. The friend replied that there was no school under the name and style of Delhi-Canada school and he was really educated in Delhi-Kannad School, a non-descript school run by a Karnataka society where his mother was a teacher. He had resorted to this prank only to impress his friends since such false boast acted as a silicone implant to give respectability to his poor schooling. It clearly reveals as to how the tag of an elite school even later in life serves an effective purpose to enhance your social status.

There was not any hope by way of bureaucratic influence and the politicians who were approached never said no but any such recommendation was always assumed to have been given just to please the individuals of their constituency and had no other useful relevance beyond that.

During the intervening period the results of the High School Examination conducted by the Maharashtra Board of Education were declared and as expected, Sharad had done exceedingly well. Dr M P Chhaya who was the then Principal of Bhartiya Vidya Bhavan was approached with the mark sheet with a hope that the problem would aleast now be solved easily. But that was not to be. Dr Chhaya said in no uncertain words that even if his ward had secured first position in the Maharashtra board examination, he was totally helpless since his own students numbering about thirty were being denied admission as there were no seats available to them in the science stream in the eleventh standard. There was a genuine feeling of helplessness and therefore it was accepted sportingly. He too was equally sad for not being helpful in admitting the child who had performed so brilliantly. As a parting gift he advised the parents that there was one Sardar Patel Vidyalaya in Lodhi Road which had reserved five seats for meritorious students migrating to Delhi from outside the state. It was rightly considered an intelligent ploy to keep the morale high of the disappointed parents since it was a tall expectation considering that the students from more than twenty states of the country would be eyeing these five seats. However, with faint hope, an application to that school was also made. A Miracle was waiting to happen. No interview of the parents or even of the child was taken, but a simple post card granting admission to the child was unexpectedly received. A right spring board was found rather by an accident than any design as such. Without any bias and prejudice it can be stated that Sardar Patel Vidyalaya continues to play a great role in instilling indomitable courage, never- die spirit and unparalled wisdom on any child whom they take under their wing. No wonder every ex-student of this institution calls himself with pride 'A Patelian'. The smooth journey from the vidyalaya to yet other prestigious institute of police training named after this great son of India bears ample testimony to our humble claim.

Results of the Senior Secondary Education as expected were equally heart-warming. By this time the practice of releasing the names of the merit list holders was discontinued to discourage unhealthy competition amongst the students. However, the names of the students obtaining highest marks in a particular subject were released to the print media for publication. Sharad had obtained ninety eight marks in biology out of one hundred and stood second in the whole of India. The only one student who was ahead of him was from a Chennai school with hundred per cent marks.

Although Sharad had taken up the medical entrance examination, the results were yet not declared. As an abundant precaution he was taken to Hindu College in the north Campus of the University for admission into Zoology (Honours) stream. It was a well-considered decision since to get admission in Delhi University is also a nightmarish experience owing to the limited number of seats available. Dr Gauba, the then Head of the Dept. of Zoology, who was overseeing the process of admission; casually ask his parents why the child was unnecessary brought for admission. The parents assuming it to be an impending signal of refusal of admission were totally demoralised. Dr Gauba however could read the frustration of the parents and informed them in a very reassuring manner that he had uttered these words only to convey that this student was sure to get a seat in the MBBS course and effort to get him Zoology course was really not needed. How true he was! He had not only qualified for a seat in the colleges of Delhi University but also for admission to Agra Medical College in UP by virtue of being a domicile of Uttar Pradesh. He had also qualified in the fifteen per cent seats available in all-India medical entrance examination and was allotted a medical college in Pondicherry. For obvious reasons he graduated from

Delhi University and the other seats were surrendered in favour of other meritorious students in the waiting list.

As a counter to the concept of the elite schools, we had come across of a news item appearing in the print media roughly a year back which also deserves an equal space. A young District Magistrate of the Tamil Nadu Cadre went to a government school for admission of his son. As the paraphernalia he travelled with was too visible, his visit did not go unnoticed and he was immediately surrounded by a battery of the press reporters who thought the Collector must have come on some routine inspection visit. To their utter surprise they found the Collector of the district standing in a queue incognito with the other parents for admission of his own son. On being questioned as to why he was admitting his son in a municipal corporation school when he could get a seat in any prestigious school he said without any aura of arrogance that if he could get into the elite cadre of the Indian Administrative Service by studying in a Government school why not his sons. We therefore, want to impress that we should not blow the unnecessary trumpet about the myth of the elite schools.

## Chapter VI

# Entry into the University College of Medical Sciences

While in government service, a public servant fears most is the possibility of transfer. All shorts of tricks, pressures, false representations, political and bureaucratic pressures are brought to get a transfer order cancelled. The reasons for such tendencies are also very obvious. Transfer entails uprooting from a well settled life to an unknown place. Residential accommodation, school admission of children, adjustment a new work culture and changed social environments are mainly responsible for such illogical and irrational attitude as these adversely affect the studies of the children.

The father of Sharad was transferred from Mumbai (then Bombay) in March, 1983 to Delhi. He could hardly afford to get the transfer order cancelled as it was ordered as a consequence of his promotion in the next higher rank which no one can refuse as promotions are not easy to come by and he unwillingly landed in Delhi. The first problem a government servant faces in Delhi is that of an official accommodation. The city was predominantly inhabited by the babus, as the govt. servant is sarcastically addressed to. The joke in these days was that if you accidentally collide with some one in the egg market, every second victim of such collision would definitely be a Deputy Secretary to the Govt. of India. In such a scenario, to expect the official accommodation where rent is highly subsidised and ridiculously low was just a wishful thinking as one may have to want for years owing to the long waiting list of the applicants for government accommodation. Private accommodation was just too costly and beyond the paying capacity of the public servant.

With lot of difficulty, father of Sharad could manage a two room tenement rented accommodation across the trans-Jamuna in East Delhi. The locality was called Mayur Vihar, a newly built Delhi Development Authority Complex, comprising of middle and lower middle class inhabitants. It was aptly called 'Mayur Vihar' as the peacocks outnumbered the human inhabitants in those days. The colony was connected to the main city by a single DTC bus while plied in the route by their own whims and fancies as they had to adjust their tea and lunch timing depending on the prevailing situation. The entire family shifted in June, 1983 after the results of High School Board Examinations were declared by the Maharashtra Board of Secondary Education. It is hereafter that the ghost of transfer started showing its colours to the new settlers in an altogether unknown city.

There was a vast difference in the educational system of Maharashtra and Delhi. In Maharashtra, there is a three language formulae and upto 10th standard one has to compulsorily study English, Hindi and any one other language from the pool of Marathi, French or German languages. Besides learning an additional language chates difficulties in your efforts in other subjects. The situation was further worsened because the admissions to 11th standards were over in the month of April of the academic calendar year. Thus, there were no seats available in any of the reputed schools.

The gravity of the disappointment can be gauged from the fact that the father of Sharad was a life member of the Bhartiya Vidya Bhawan Society with headquarters in Bombay and was carrying a favourable recommendatory letter from a top functionary of the society for admission of his son in 11th standard in Bhartiya Vidya Bhawan located on Curzon Road. Needless to say the school was run by the Bhartiya Vidya Bhawan Society and Dr M.P. Chhaya, the Principal of the school, found it too difficult to accommodate Sharad since his own students numbering approximately thirty who had studied in the school from the very childhood were displaced with advised to took school admission elsewhere.

The sanguine advice from Dr Chhaya, the Principal of the school, was however very encouraging that admission of Sharad be tried in Sardar Patel Vidyalaya in Lodhi Road who had five seats reserved for the monotonous students coming from other states of India. On the face of it, it did not appear to be a very hopeful alternative because five seats were too few to accommodate the monotonous students of roughly two dozen states who may have migrated to the city.

Luck as one may call it, the extraordinary achievements of Sharad in High School exam enabled him to get a seat in Sardar Patel Vidyalaya, one of the best schools in these days. It was really a matter of real joy and pride too to get the ward admitted

*Yalk ride in Shimla the Year 1991*

in the school. The frustrations of failure of efforts in the past few months which was nothing short of a nightmare disappeared soon.

There are factors in life which we can neither visualise nor anticipate. No sooner was the crisis of school admission was over another distressing episode followed.

As stated in this chapter, Mayur Vihar was a newly developed colony and had no infrastructure in place to ensure healthy living. For a population of few thousands, there was only one Doctor Luthria and that too he was a new entrant in the profession after obtaining his MBBS degree. Sharad developed a strange disease and his both hands were affected with boils as if someone had dipped his hands in hot boiling water. These boils would burst automatically giving a place for a new boils to appear. Dr Luthria found the problem beyond his competence and referred the case to a skin specialist who was a retired professor of Dermatology from Maulana Azad Medical College. Surprising there was no precept table improvement in his condition. It was not only irritating but humiliating too for a child since his own classmates would discreetly avoid him. Besides, his studies were adversely hampered.

His parents sought the guidance from one of their family friends who inadvertently took an appointment from one Dr Caroli, who incidentally was an eminent cardiologist and honorary physician to President of India besides being a Padma Bhushan awardee. He was practicing medicine privately in East Patel Nagar. Dr Caroli was totally surprised and got irritated, of course with no visible signs when comforted with the patient afflicted with skin ailment. He regained his cool and said that since the patient was referred by one of his very close friends, he would definitely attend to him. He carried out a number of pathological tests which could not lead him to any definite diagnosis. He therefore, ordered a special test which was casting Rs 500 a real fortune in those days. He diagnosed that

*Being congratulated by Dr Malhotra Vice-chancellor Shimla University after being awarded first prize in Hindi Essay and English Short Story Competition organised by 'LEKHNI 88' an in house magazine of Indira Gandhi Medical College Shimla where Doctors of Medical College of North India Participated.*

the patient was suffering from allergy animal protein and advised complete stoppage of consumption of meat, chicken, eggs and fish for 18 months. He prescribed some simple medicines which looked like white granules of sugar to be taken for three months. Needless to say the boils disappeared within a few days never to appear in life again. The most satisfying aspect of his treatment was that now he enjoys animal proteins with no signs of any discomfort. The whole episode speaks volume about the competence of our medical fraternity and they deserve our salute.

It goes to the credit of Sharad that inspite of loosing very important academic periods, he cleared the 11th standard with flying colours just by seer grit and determination. He was thus treated with respect and admiration by his fellow class student. Smt Vibha Parthsarathy, the then Principal of the school was highly impressed by his performance and he soon became the blue-eyed boy of the principal. Impressed by the performance of Sharad, she offered a seat to his sister in Sardar Patel Vidyalaya who had just cleared the 10th standard from the Delhi Board and was a student of the Bhartiya Vidya Bhwan. The co-author of this book is the student whom we are referring as sister of Sharad. The logic of Vibha Parthsarathy was too simple and it was if Sharad was so brilliant his sister could not be far behind. The opportunity was grabbed with both hands without giving any second thoughts.

The almighty has strange and cruel ways to test your strength of your character forbearance. Sharad was now in 12th standard, a very crucial academic year where your performance indicates fairly accurately as to in which professional field you are likely to enter. Unfortunately, he again fell ill. By this time, Dr S.K. Gupta an MD had established his clinic in Mayur Vihar. Dr Gupta diagnosed that Sharad was suffering from typhoid as well as jaundice and needed immediate hospitalisation. Since his father was not yet issued card under Central Government Health Scheme, he was admitted in a private facility called B L Kapoor Hospital in Pusa Road which was roughly 20 kilometers away from their residence. In these days B.L. Kapoor Hospital was just a nursing home and it is learnt now that it has grown into a referred hospital. It was a very complicated medical case and needed constant monitoring. The decision to admit him was a blessing in disguise since father of Dr S.K. Gupta had just retired from the post of Professor of Paedriatic medicine in PGI Rohtak and settled in Delhi, made it a point to be with Sharad to monitor his condition. The kind gesture was unsolicited and without any monetary considerations. It was just a benevolent gesture because he just wanted to remain abreast of the developments in the medical field.

By the time, he was discharged from the hospital he was virtually reduced to a skeleton. His parent's thoughts that it was prudent to advice Sharad that he should drop the

Senior Secondary Board Examination as any undue strain may adversely affect the recuperation but he stubbornly refused. He did appear in the final examination and came out with flying colours so much so that he scored 98 marks out of 100 in the biology and stood second to a student of Madras in all-India merit in this particular subject. He later conveyed to his parents that answer to the two marks question missed by him was known to him as it was a very simple question answer to which was known to him as for back when he was in 8th standard in St. Xavir High School, Bombay but he could not recollect that at the material time when needed. We were never witness to the incident but prophecy of still rings in our ears when Dr Gauba, Professor and Head of the Zoology, Department where he was seeking admission in the BSc Honour stream remarked that he was unnecessarily brought for admission since if he could not qualify for the medical entrance examination, no body would be able to qualify.

One thing we have never been able to understand that he never contemplated to appear in any other field of professional courses entrance examination other than the medicine. Engineering would have been much easier for him as a large number of seats are on the offer. He refused to even fill up the entrance examination as he was convinced of his abilities.

In retrospect we can reconstruct his thought process. It appears that as he was perpetually falling sick in the crucial year. He preferred the medical stream since he did not want that the effort of other aspiring and talented students be stunted due to such unexpected ailments in future and to ensure that it was but necessary to become a medical doctor. Yet, another point also need clarification as to why he appeared in the board examination was that in Delhi state one can take up the examination for MBBS degree only if you have passed 11th and 12th standards from a school located within the municipal corporation limit. To drop a year meant longer number of applicants in future eyeing for or taking competitive entrance examination in the medical stream. A divided attention may have adversely affected his road map.

In those days there were only three medical colleges in Delhi state and these were Maulana Azad Medical College (MAMC) with 200 seats, University College of Medical Sciences (UCMS) with 100 seats and Lady Harding Medical College exclusively for the girl students with only 100 seats. In effect, there were less than 300 seats for boys as the girl students equally brilliant always made deep inroads into the quota of the boys by securing high ranking in the merit list. To be doubly sure of the success Sharad also appeared in the pre-medical list of Utter Pradesh being a domicile of the state besides for the medical college seat in Pondicherry being a union territory.

The competitive examinations are altogether different cup of tea because there is nothing like qualifying per centage. The admission is assured only on your position in the merit list and seats available. Thus, one can never be certain of the admission. Surprising no such procedure of entrance tests was in vogue in Maharashtra at least in those days, and one could get into medicine or engineering stream depending on your position in the merit list of Senior Secondary School examination of the Maharashtra Board.

As parents of Sharad did not want that he should get frustrated in the event of not qualifying in the entrance examination of pre-medical test examination, a close friend and colleague of Sharad's father named, Shevendra Singh Rana volunteered to check the list of successful candidates which was also displayed in Safdarjung Hospital. Shri Rana broke the happy news of higher ranking in the merit list where he stood at 64th position. It was indeed creditable as he had lost valuable academic periods in the school owing to his sickness and further it was curtain that owing to his fragile health on account of intermittent sickness must have put lot of constraints on his efforts by his own standards.

As the saying goes that fortune favours the brave he simultaneously qualified in pre-medical test for admission in to government medical colleges run by the UP government beside Pondicherry. These seats were surrendered in favour of equally talented aspirants who were wait listed concerned medical colleges were not satisfied with plain letter of surrender and an affidavit was insisted upon. Only on submitted of such an affidavit the formality of the surrender was treated as final, sometimes problem of plenty too is equally taxing. And finally, Sharad took the admission in the UCMS.

Apparently with no plausible justification students preferred MAMC and he would have easily got into the college owing to his high ranking in the merit list, UCMS was preferred as a first choice the primary reason being the proximity of the medical college from the residence as by this time was allotted an out of turn official accommodation owing to compelling and genuine compassionate grounds. The medical college was then attached to Safdar Jung Hospital barely three kilometers away and could be reached even by walking if one so desired.

The other reason was that there was only one other college by that name and it was University College of Medical Sciences, London. The intake of entrants was also restricted unlikely that of MAMC where the teaching faculty member had to use public address system to teach the students where the class room gave the impression as if an election rally was being addressed. In the UCMS in comparison of the MAMC. Financially, the college had more resources since it was part of the Delhi University which entitled to education grants provided by the University Grants Commission besides usual quota of financial aid provided by the Delhi Government administration. Commuting to the college too was easy and comfortable in comparison to MAMC. Sharad had migrated from Bombay where the public discipline using the public transport is really commendable. You cannot jump the queue to board the public transport bus. Conductor would not allow you to get into the bus. Delhi is just opposite. You not only require a robust physique but also an athletic temperament to get into a bus falling which one is likely to get stranded in a bus stops for hours together. Public discipline is thus of vital importance by the using of the state transport as you are at-least sure of reaching your destination in time and it also enables you to conserve your energy and you do not get unduly tired when you reach your destination.

Sometimes the behaviour of certain politicians in a bizarre fashion is too difficult to understand. An influential politician holding a cabinet rank in the union government in thought it prudent to shift the medical college to the trans-Jamuna area approximately 40 km. away from its present location. A new hospital named Guru Teg Bahadur Hospital besides teaching and hostel blocks were newly constructed and the UCMS was shifted to its new location by the end of December, 1985. It is not that there was not necessity for a hospital and medical college in the area but it was the manner and style besides motive which was the prime consideration of such move. A medical college with equally high standards could have been started even with fewer intake of students than to demolish well functioning infrastructure completely. Public is too intelligent to understand the reasons of such illogical decisions. The whole exercise was to win the sympathy of the voters of east Delhi who got alienated from him owing to his suspect role in anti-Sikh mob in 1984. Such negative tricks for personal gains at the cost of existing and well-oiled teaching institutions can only be deplored. The advantage which Sharad enjoyed owing to the close proximity of the college was completely lost.

The real test of an intellectual lies in the fact as to how an individual converts his disadvantages into a huge advantage. That is what we shall witness now. The distance of the medical college which was within the walking distance was two hours bus journey now. Unlike the facility of advantage of university special buses provided by the Delhi Transport Corporation to the north campus, no facility of that kind was available to the medical colleges. There was no alternative but a golden opportunity was available to enhance the physical endurance by relying on the state bus services in east Delhi was then a really a neglected area owing to its typical lower middle class population structure. Although as a student, he was provided an independent room in the hostel, he never stayed there owing to his emotional attachment to his mother and preferred to commute daily continuously for a period of four academic years in the college. There was some relief to his physical torture during the internship period when perforced he had to stay in the hostel.

His parents believed in strict fiscal discipline owing to the constraints imposed on them being a fixed salaried class. To seek some relief from the taxing regime of the college he requested his parents that the family take a deserving holiday and visit some hill station. As expected his request was turned down politely however an option was given to take effect that in case such holiday was necessitated as a result of some academic activities the family could afford to enjoy the luxury of well earned respite.

Sharad was on the look out to discover such an opportunity and it knocked at the door sooner than expected. Indira Gandhi Medical College in Shimla invited entry in Hindi Essay and English short story from the medical students of the college located in north India for their in-house magazine LEKHAN-88 with an offer that the winning candidates will be awarded the prizes in person by the Vice Chancellor of the Shimla University. Although Sharad was a laborious student, he was not altogether a book worm. He devoted considerable time in extra curriculum activities more so in creative writing, without the knowledge of his parents he forwarded his entries in both the categories for consideration of the editorial board of the magazine. As he had expected, he got the first prize in both the categories and was invited to collect the prizes. It was probably the first and the last pleasure trip during his medical studies which the entire family enjoyed at his cost by planning a short holiday in and around Shimla.

Although no one had a background of experience in the medical field in the family, he did exceedingly well in his batch. He soon become a blue eyed student of the teaching faculty and during the internship, he was occasionally assigned to take the classes of new entrants of the first and second year students whenever some faculty member was unable to take a class owing to the unexpected emergency commitments. Such an arrangement was put in place to ensure that the idle student did not create a nuisance by playing pranks with each other. A very interesting incident took place during this period which cannot escape our attention and we would like to share with our readers.

During one of these period of his internship he contacted very high fever and to cure himself he prescribed the medicines himself. Unfortunately the temperature did not subside and he could not go to the college. Noticing his absence from the hospital, his very close friend and class fellow Dr Pawan Bhargava visited him in his residence in RK Puram locality with a bouquet of roses and get well soon message. After examining him and the line of treatment, he simply said to his mother and we quote, "Auntie there is nothing wrong with him clinically and he is simply a victim of some evil eyes, specially girl students because they constantly look at him without battling an eyelid for his extra-ordinary proficiency on the subject. No treatment was needed and some rituals as resorted to in any household in pursuance of the grandmothers advice will do the trick to cure him." The advise was religiously implemented. His mother did some rituals with few herbs, salt and red chilies and offered the same to the fire god. In colloquial language this well established practice is called "Nazar Utarna" (casting away evil focus) and within twenty four hours he was back to his college. The traditional belief is that even the look of admiration at owns kith and kin, well wishers and admirers can cause such disturbances which is called *"Apno ki Nazar"*

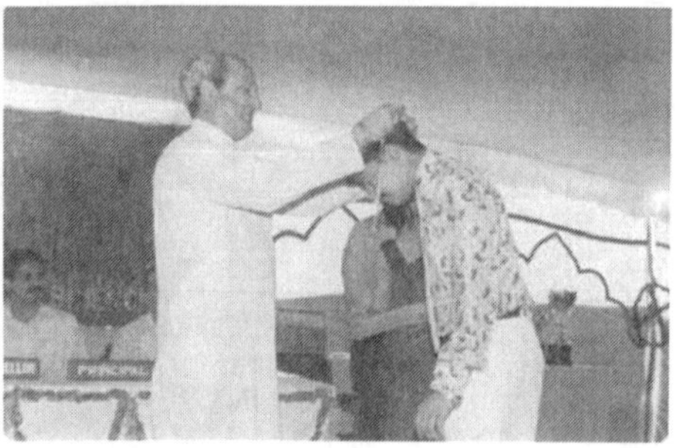

*Being awarded Gold Medal by the Lt Governor Shri Bhandari for Topping in Obstretics and Gynaecology in the Delhi University. He Passed his MBBS Course with Honours and Destinations.*

loosely translated that would mean ill-effects of own affectionate looks. We have no answers to questions which may be raised about the efficacy of traditional wisdom of grand-mothers but Dr Pawan Bhargava is definitely a very successful practicing doctor in the United Kingdom.

As expected Sharad graduated in Medicine from the UCMS in the year, 1990 with honours and distinction. He topped in Microbiology, preventive and social medicine, ophthalmology and university gold medalist in obstetrics and gynaecology.

# Chapter VII

# And the Prophecy Comes True

In Bombay Customs where the father of Sharad was initially posted in 1971, one Dr Naval Kishore Sharma was also serving. The gentlemen was highly accomplished academically as he was a post graduate in Hindi Literature, Sanskrit Literature and English literatures besides held the PhD degree can astronomy from the Bombay University. He was posted in the Bombay Customs commiserate as a Raj Bhasha Adhikari (Official Language Officer) popularly known as Hindi Officer. He had also interest in making the horoscopes, his family occupation for the last three generations in east Delhi.

We all know when a child is born in any family, the parents approach the priest to know the future of the child. The priests are invariably too generous in forecasting the future of a child. We do not know how scientific an art it is but to keep the fortune seeker in a good humour they always predict a very rosy picture about the future of the child. Dr Sharma had a deep-rooted faith in the religion in which he was born and had very fugal and pious life. Strange it may seem but it is on record that he refused a posting in Indian Embassy in Washington as he thought that he will not be able to adjust in an alien western culture however later accepted an assignment as the second secretary (Culture) in the Indian Embassy in Mauritius.

Dr Sharma was a very good friend of Sharad's father as both were of Literary inclinations. Out of sheer curiosity he was requested to forecast the future of the child. The detailed date, time, month and year were given to him to facilitate his task. Usually the fortune tellers predict the future in generic terms and never commit them to any specific occurrences in life. After taking into consideration the planetary positions at the time of birth of the child and making certain calculations he predicted that the child will be an Indian Police Service Officer one day. Without showing any visual disagreement to Dr Sharma, the parents concluded that the prediction was simply a easy way to please his friend. The physical attributes of the child did not show any indication that he would opt for a career in an uniformed service. Further, he had yet not cleared his fifth standard in a primary section of the school.

In due course of time, Dr Sharma was transferred to Delhi and by sheer coincidence the father of Sharad too in the same station. In due course of time, Sharad qualified in the medical entrance examination and joined the University College of Medical Sciences in Delhi University for his MBBS degree. Although he had simultaneously qualified for admission to UP medical colleges by virtue of being the domicile of the state as well as to the medical college in Pondicherry on the basis of All India Entrance Examination for admission into medical college. Out of sheer curiosity, Dr Sharma was approached with a request whether he would like to modify his earlier prediction in the light of the present developments. To their utter surprise Dr Sharma continued to believe that his prediction could not go wrong. After the MBBS degree Sharad also cleared the post graduate entrance examination for the degree of Master of Surgery (Opthalmology) and allotted PGI Chandigarh to pursue the course. Simultaneously, he had taken up All India Medical Entrance Examination and was allotted the northern railway for an appointment as Resident Medical Officer in due course. Apparently, the parents were too happy and proud with the extraordinary achievements of their son. We do not know as to what prompted them to approach Dr Sharma again as to what he had to say about his prophecy. It appears that their inflated ego had motivated them to approach Dr Sharma to remind him how wrong he was in his predictions. This time Dr Sharma who was popularly called the Brahmarishi (the supreme sage) in bureaucratic circles lost his cool and tensely replied "please wait and see". The matter ended then and there insofar as the parents were concerned their curiosity as to how it could happen remained unanswered.

Although the formative years of Sharad were spent amidst the bureaucratic people around yet he never seemed to have been influenced by the glamour and authority exercised by them. He appeared to be of the opinion that the salary offered to them was really a peanut in comparison to the expectations from them as professional managers of the administrative institutions. It was partly true because he had seen his father leading a frugal life style and yet was perpetually in a financial crises. It was really very true in early nineteen's. He opted for the railway job because he wanted to help his parents financially and kept the post graduation in science in the back burner. It was in late eighty's, the younger sister of Sharad was studying in Miranda House, a college in north campus of the Delhi University and pursuing her post graduation in zoology. She used to return home by evening with voluminous books on the subject which were issued only to the senior teaching faculty members. A close friend of his father was a Reader in Delhi University and thus the facility of constant access to these rare reading materials through his courtesy was really a boon. Sharad was sitting idle at home waiting for the appointment later he inadvertently got hooked to these books.

On one fine morning, he approached his father with a one liner request whether he could appear in the civil services examination. His father gave him a hard look as he was aware of the fact that he had never studied any subject which could be opted in the civil services examination. To appear in the examination one had to have at least honours level knowledge of a particular subject to have some remote chances of success. In those years the medical subjects were not included in the scheme of option of subjects. To his parents it appeared something like day dreaming as the cream of the bright students of 176 universities besides students of IIT's and engineering college across the country used to aspire to get into the elite civil services. In spite of these facts his father hesitatingly agreed with him and gave consent to go ahead as he did not want to curb or frustrate his intellectual inclinations or ambitions. On being probed as to what subjects he would opt in the examination, without giving any second thoughts he simply said any subject like sociology, anthropology and zoology etc.

The ball was now in the court of his father since as a fall out of his decision, another insurmountable problem cropped in. The prospectus for the appointment in the railway clearly stipulated that those who are selected will have to execute a bond binding themselves to pay three lacs to the govt, in case they left the service within five years of their appointment. Assuming that he will succeed the problem was from where the money will come from as and when the term and conditions are enforced for leaving the railway service prematurely. The only viable option his father thought was to keep the option of joining, the railway service be kept alive in case of unfavourable outcome in the civil service examination. It was considered expedient to ensure the letter of the appointment by the railway was held in abeyance for a year. He did succeed in his designs and the file from where the appointment letter was to be issued was declared as misplaced. The dealing officer although obliged his father by conceding to his request was realty astonished to understand the motive of such a request and that too from the father of a successful candidate. Surprisingly, the appointment letter has yet not seen the light of the day even after two decades and may be some one finds it in the archives of the Railway Board one day.

This peculiar and bizarre incident could not escape the attention of the President presiding the interview board of the Union Public Service Commission. With some hidden purpose in his mind asked Dr Sharad "do you think that the railway board is all that inefficient so as not to issue you the single appointment letter for a duration of one year." The reply too was equally clever from Sharad who politely replied "How do I know sir, I am only an unemployed youth." Developments hereafter are all known to us. The prophecy or the blessings whatever you may prefer to call it from an enlighten Brahmin had came true. We all are the script writers of our destiny but how shall the story emerge is beyond our understanding.

## Chapter VIII

# Over to the National Police Academy

When you are on a National Highway to reach your destination, you have the option to skirt townships en-route by using the bye-pass. However, you can never ignore the existence of a city or its landmarks thereof and these appear in your mental horizon. We definitely did not want to include this chapter in our original concept because we did not relish the idea that our effort should give the impression of compilation of confidential reports about the author.

Notwithstanding our plan it was not feasible to avoid it completely. To reach a destination one has to measure the entire

*After Mounting the Horse named* PRIYA *in (National Police Academy)? or was in Mussorrie.*

length of the distance with no choice of being choosy. We shall therefore, confine ourself to the incidents and events which are in public domain and therefore we intend to present the birds eye view of his achievements in the Police Academy but more importantly his entry into the Punjab Cadre.

During the early ninetees Punjab was in the grip of terrorism and he was allotted the Punjab Cadre. His mother was very apprehensive of the happenings in the state and she did not relish the idea that her only son should face the daunting challenges in the early stage of his carrier. His opinion got further cemented when she learnt that one of her distant relative who had got into the IAS and was allotted Punjab Cadre, manipulated to get his cadre changed to Madhya Pradesh state only because of the problem of the terrorism. There was no urgency for a job according to his mother since he had already qualified for the post of a class one service as a doctor on the basis of All India Medical Entrance Examination and was waiting for the appointment letter. But father of Sharad had an altogether different perception and his arguments forced the mother to change her rigid opinion and agreed to allow him to join the Punjab Cadre as an IPS Officer. There is a very interesting story behind this radical change in her perception and does need mention. The story runs like this.

A prominent syndicate of gold smugglers from Pakistan was operating from Ferozepur city in Punjab. The contraband yellow metal used to be shifted to Delhi and secreted in an unknown godown for onward transportation to Mumbai by road. The modus operandi was so fool proof and impregnable as all efforts to neutralise the syndicate failed in Delhi. Father of Sharad who was heading an intelligence outfit in Delhi was therefore directed to shift his base to Ferozepur and trail the carriers by road right upto Delhi to get the requisite break-through.

The situation in Punjab was rather too grave to undertake such an ambitious mission. Ferozepur is a small town and people know each other at least by face if not by name, usually private vehicles are used for such operations but the Taxi operators of Delhi refused to co-operate as they did not want their drivers to expose the risk of loss of limb or life in a terrorist affected state. There was no option but to use the government ambassador cars which cannot go unnoticed even from a distance. The timely assistance of Punjab Police was however a welcome relief. They blocked a complete hotel for the officers. In those days even the private hotels never displayed their identity sign boards, no guest registers were maintained, no bills for payments for boarding and lodging were ever presented. So much so that even cigarette ashtrays were found missing in the guest rooms.

The entire team used to get down atleast two kilometers away from the vehicle before entering the Municipal Corporation limit of Ferozepur and walk to the hotel in a batches of two's or three's with their luggage. The driver of the car was instructed to proceed to the city. The Punjab Police had designated a parking place for our vehicles to ensure the secrecy of the mission. It was a very unusual parking place which one can imagine. It was Ferozepur general hospital where hundreds of used and damaged cars were dumped and the drivers were told to keep the vehicles hidden from the public view by parking the vehicles amid those discarded cars. The entire credit for the smooth operation goes to Shri Ajit Singh, IPS who was the then DIG of Ferozepur range for his foresight planning and execution. In reality he was the de facto leader of the whole secret mission.

For some unknown reasons, probably owing to some bottlenecks in the flow of consignments from the Pakistan side the intelligence did not fructify and therefore in spite of a week long vigil the team was recalled to Delhi. The team accordingly left Ferozepur in early morning hours one day. While they were somewhere between Ferozepur and Mandi Dabwali, there cars were stopped on the road by few farmers who advised the unknown occupants of the vehicles to go back to Ferozepur city as a strong team of terrorist was waiting in an ambush only a few kilometers away. The team was also advised to undertake the journey in broad day light; when the terrorist will disappear in the thin air. Their gesture was fraught with danger with complete disregard to their own safety who were more eager to save life of those to whom they had never known or seen or had no vested interests whatsoever.

Sharad was getting full feedback of these happenings and it only strengthened his resolve to excel in the training in the Police Academy. Needless to say, he acquitted himself exceedingly well, was adjudged the best overall officer of his batch and was awarded Prime Minister baton and Home Minister revolver on the completion of training in the academy. It was not an end of his exploits in the academy. He was the first medical doctor to command the parade in the Police Academy. The icing on the cake was that he commanded not only his own batch but also of one batch junior Probationary Officers since their course was so structured that they had to pass out along-with their senior batch. His batch was also the one which got an academic degree of Master of Police Administration as the academy was affiliated to the Osmania University for the purpose. Unfortunately, the practice appears to have been discontinued after the passing out of his batch. The question of leadership ingrained him by the National Police Academy continues to motivate him in his day-to-day policing activities and he is now the recipient of the President's Medal for Meritorious and Distinguished Service which was awarded to him in the year 2010 on the occasion of Republic Day of India.

# Chapter IX

# Police Force - An Outsider's View

As biographers, when we conceptualised the outline of the book to give a shape of own views, we were fully conscious that we would abstain from commenting on the functioning of the police force. The reasons which influenced our thinking were two fold. Firstly, we honestly found that we were really deficient even in our rudimentary knowledge of the functioning of the police force to navigate our route anywhere though the subject and secondly, numerous police commissions to reform the functioning and improve the image of the

*And with Shri Atal Bihari Bajpai the then Prime Minister of India who was on his visit to Moga (Punjab) to address a rally.*

department had already deliberated on the subject and furnished their reports to the government. Thus, it was considered prudent not to involve where even angels fear to tread. We, however, compelled to revise our approach because our indifference to these vital questions may even raise questions on our own intellectual integrity. We are fully aware that we have no expertise on the subject but as a common citizen, we definitely have a ringside view of the problem because it impacts our day-to-day life.

No one can deny the fact that the police organisation is the only arm of the governance which is accountable to plethora of agencies which keep a very close watch on its performance. They are answerable to each and every single common man of the society, human rights commission, anti-corruption bodies besides are also under surveillance by their own vigilance mechanism. Then there is a police complain authority which is although not constituted uniformly in all the states of the union. Besides public at large is equally very proactive highlighting the alleged culpabilities of the force. Such safeguards, however, exist virtually all over the world because the police have the prerogative to kill or incapacitate an individual in performance of their bonafide duties. However, owing to numerous unforeseen contingencies the police do cross the limit which result in excesses but it does not give us a license to demoralise the force accusing them of misdemeanor, dereliction of duty or brutality because it falls in the preview of the government who are disciplinary authority of their force.

We are neither socio-economic scientists nor the political master's therefore we shall confine ourselves only to most visible facts of the conduct of the police scene as a common citizen. These observations are not based on any scientific study or analysis of data but are purely hypothetical and product of our common sense. In our view the alleged conception and brutality of the force are two main factors which dent their creditability and tarnish their image. If these two monsters are contained even if not eliminated more than half battle is won.

Let us take the case of corruption first and understand how it germinates. In addition to the sharp decline in social values, the inadequacy of the police force contributes equally to corruption. Fortunately, we came across aneditorial appearing in the Hindi Daily *Punjab Kesari* at 4th November, 2014 which made a job rather easy. As we all know that the police establishment is one side but most important side of the coin of judicial system of any civilised society, yet it is beyond our comprehension to fathom as to why the police is most neglected organisation of the government. Our Hon'ble Supreme Court in its judgment in November, 2006 had passed certain orders for the structural changes in the police department but all that remains unimplemented. Even the then Home Minister P. Chidambaram had admitted that our police structure is old and outdated the police personnel are poorly equipped with its outdated weaponry. Training for career progression is virtually non-existent which in due course of time gets reflected in poor policing resulting in increase in crime.

It is an open secret that the organisation and methods directorate which evaluates the requirement of police personnel is very conservative in its approach even then existing vacancies are never filled. The shortfall in the strength of police personnel is too glaring to go unnoticed and we are quoting from the editorial cited above in respect of few states which is tabulated as under :-

| *Sr. No.* | *State* | *Sanctioned Strength* | *Working strength* | *Vacancies* |
|---|---|---|---|---|
| 1. | Indian Union State Goa | 22,09,027 | 16,60,666 | 5,48,361 |
| 2. | Uttar Pradesh | - | - | 1,01,100 |
| 3. | Gujarat | - | - | 45,191 |
| 4. | West Bengal | - | - | 38,725 |
| 5. | Andhra Pradesh | - | - | 32,247 |
| 6. | Chattishgarh | - | - | 20,670 |

*In Full Ceremonial Dress in Maharaja Ranjit Singh Punjab Police Academy Phillaur (Punjab) while saving as Director of the Academy.*

Uttar Pradesh has the maximum shortfall in the sanctioned strength and unfortunately in the supervisory cadre as there is shortfall of 50 per cent in Head Constable ranks, 57 per cent in Sub-Inspectors rank, 73 per cent in Inspectors rank.

Such inapproprate ratio of police personnel vis-a-vis the population of the state results in long hours of work, sedentary life and frustration. No wonder, there is rise in obesity and cardiovascular diseases in the police forces which generates frustration, lack of focus, and short cuts of easy way of earning money and breeds brutality with a view to achieve quicker results. In fact, obesity is frustrating all walks of life. In army they have coined a dignified phrase to describe it and call it tendency to put on weight. Any officer or jawan having such tendency is put an adverse annual confidence report to apply course correction to his life style. We feel police too should invent some ingenuity to fight the menace.

The police have a very vast area to maintain law and order but their deployed strength does not commensurate with the task in hand. The man in uniform becomes casual and indifferent to the task assigned to him and falls easy prey to the monetary inducement. We Indians worship the goddess of the wealth and welcome it specially when she walks in voluntarily.

Let us illustrate it with a real incident, we have approximately 600 kilometer sea coast line in Maharashtra. There are approximately two lacs fishing crafts/boats who venture out to sea for fishing every day and return every evening. The Fishing deptt. has no control over them as they wash off their hands after granting license for fishing activities. The customs have no infrastructure to mount any worthwhile surveillance in them. The police had no presence or role of policing and thus field is left open to antisocial, antinational modules. A mother ship comes close to Indian coast and launches its small craft laden with RDX near Alibagh on Konkan coast and disappears in thin air. The RDX is taken to Bombay city in ten brand new ambassador cars. The results thereof are too horrifying to recapitulate, the Bombay serial blast in 1993 resulting into loss of hundreds of innocent life can never get obliterated from our memory. The primary reason for this ghastly crime was the result of the inadequacy of the police force as well as that of customs who were forced to believe that only washing powder had landed. The customs preferred to pocket just few lacs which was negotiated and paid to them in a New Mumbai air conditioned restaurant. No enforcement agency ever tried to check the veracity of the information as it entailed division of their own depleted strength of manpower. The temptation of easy money was too tempting to resist. This untold story was revealed to our source by an accused senior customs officer serving his life term who was out on a short parole. Lately, the Maharashtra police is now creating coastal police stations to monitor illegal activities in sea coasts.

The second main reason which breeds corruption is that we as citizens have no respect for law; our basic philosophy is that laws are meant to be broken and it is our great privilege to indulge in such passion. Unfortunately, knowledgeable or the ignorant, high and low, and poor or the rich all have a common penchant to break the law. The manifestation of such attitude is too visible in traffic violations. Many may not be aware that the road accident victims resulting in their death account for more than any single killer disease in India. Few years back a cabinet minister's wife was killed at Motibagh crossing in South Delhi while going to airport simply because the VIP driver jumped the red light and had a head on collision with an incoming vehicle. The lady died on the spot. When you visit cities like Hong Kong or Singapore, you will never find a police constable regulating the traffic. Jumping a red light signal is unheard off. Drivers changing lanes and blowing horn are treated with the contempt they deserve. Things do not end there. We bribe the traffic man to escape the challans and boast of our resourcefulness over a glass of wine in the evening to our friends. In traffic offences it is the road user who is to be blamed because he is the sole reason and perennial source to promote the culture of bribe.

The second major allegation against the police force is that they are brutal while discharging their duties. There appears to be some truth in the allegation that they resort to third degree methods but no one wants to go into the reasons thereof. We tend to forget that the policeman is running against time. He cannot keep an accused in police custody for more than 24 hours and has to produce him before a magistrate or release him. A hardened criminal or a anti-national culprit is not a coffee vending machine that you insert the coin, press the button and your cup is filled with instant coffee. He feels helpless and resorts to third degree methods. Why does no one take a bold step to amend the criminal procedure code in a manner that the legitimate rights of the accused and end of justice are not at cross purposes? Even in the United States police self-styled human rights activist use such inhuman methods as the pathetic condition of their detention camps and the treatment they are subjected to amply demonstrate is it not possible to revisit Cr.PC on the subject ?

The policeman should evoke our sympathy than disdain. The growing charter of their duties due to spurt in crime, insurgents threats, deteriorating value system of the society at large and added burden of VVIP security results in long duty hours without adequate rest, lack of amenities and undue stress take a toll of their mental as well as physical health. All these cumulative factors lead to corruption and brutality since it is the only escape route available to them.

At this point in career, Sharad has worked closely in all the police departments. One thing very peculiar about him and a very healthy sign indeed is that he believes leading his team from the front instead of being an ivory tower officer. A highly knowledged officer, he rightly believe in the Chinese proverb which says that the true essence of knowledge is having known it, apply it. In his own way he continues to engage himself constantly to improve the image of the department. Hard work, discipline, unbiased mind and an impeccable integrity are the weapons of his armour and it is very satisfying to see him standing tall.

## Chapter X

# National Security Strategy- A Jettisoned Concept

Certain words in English language are very fascinating owing to their import, connotation and interpretations. Even if we are not conscious of their impact in our thinking and behaviour these words have percolated deep into own psyche and deeply affect our thinking. We find the word "strategy" in this category. Our intention is not to go into etymology or its definition since it means different things to each individuals, depending on one's perception while defining the road map of the journey or blueprint of their goals in life. Such tendencies are not only characteristic of an individual but are too visible even in a group, society or even a nation.

Each individual in society is knowingly or unknowingly guided by his own strategic considerations to enhance his economic security and status in the social structure. Be it a poor farmer holding a tiny piece of land, professionals in the field of academics, medicine or engineering, all endeavour to seek the excellence and ultimate goals of life with the help of their own strategic perceptions.

The journey of the development of the strategic concepts itself is a very interesting subject. To safeguard against the dangers to their life against predatory animals the man invented tools made of stones, bows and arrows. To survive the hazards of inhospitable weather conditions he learnt to dress himself with barks of trees and skins of the killed animals. With the development of the science and technology, more sophisticated precepts of strategical thinking also evolved with the passage of time.

The first manifestations of the strategic precepts we witness in the pre-historic times as narrated in our purana's (mythological historical compilations) the society in those days comprised of two rival cultural groups namely, Deva's (divine) and Asuras (Devils). The asuras were said to be very violent and ruthless and constantly posed a threat to the existence of devas. The divine forces therefore decided to churn the ocean in search of nectar to become immortal. They lured and successfully associated the devil forces in their gigantic effort. They were however given the head side of the snake god Vasuki which was acting as a rope. The divine cultural group thught that even if they found the nectar, the devil forces would be near unconscious owing to the constant poisonous breath of the snake and would not be in a mental state to claim any right over the joint discovery. They did find the nectar but before they could lay any claim, a beautiful lady called Mohini, planted by the devas appears in the scene and disappeared in thin air with the earthen pot containing the nectar. The whole drama was enacted after weighing numerous pross and cons of well thought strategy.

Even the classification of the social structure within the Hindu society, is the scheme of well thought strategy. A particular group appropriated the role of learning for themselves and started calling themselves Brahmins and other groups allotted different roles according to their capabilities. To begin with the classification of groups was not rigid but in due course of time it assumed the nature of *varna vywastha* (classification of castes) the ill-effects of which are too visible in the structure of modern society.

Even in the epic war between Ram and Ravana in Treta Yug (may be 3500 years before Christ). We find excellent display of strategic thinking. It was essentially a war between two cultural groups. Ravana being the king of the devil forces. He indulged in rampant killing and destruction of institutions of excellence in Aryavarta to promote his culture. The situations were created to carry the war to door step of the king of devils to ensure no collateral damage was done to the assets of divine forces in the war. We find strange similarity in war efforts of the United States in the middle east where the theatres of war are located thousand of miles away from their own homeland.

Krishna, the Yadava king of Yadav dynasty having kingdom at present day Mathura was constantly harassed by Jarasandha, the king of Magadh empire at Pataliputra (present day Patna) that he had to shift his kingdom to Dwarka and then only he could succeed to eliminate his arch enemy with the rival faction of Kuru dynasty ironically called Pandavas.

In modern days recorded history only Chanakya appears to be the master strategician who succeeded in creating the concept of modern India by his out of the box thinking and ruthless implication of his thoughts and succeeded in installing Chandragupta an unknown historical reality to be called the Maurya dynasty. After the fall of Maurya empire India got fragmented into tiny states who fought amongst themselves and the concept of strategy virtually appears to have disappeared both in precept and practice. The main reasons for such decline are attributable to the education system introduced by the Britishers who ruled India roughly two centuries. They only needed helping tools to perpetuate their rule and thinking on sensitive subjects of national security whether internal or external was the sole prerogative of the rulers. We do not find any material during the period of British rule which could germinate the seeds of military strategy or strategic thinking on internal security which could give an impetus to such thinking which could undermine their authority. It was the sole prerogative of the rulers only and none else.

The fleeting reference to our history was essential that although it was ingrained in our blood but it was sucked out by the foreign rulers for their own selfish interests.

In the present day scenario a vital question needs a very urgent and honest answer. Firstly, can a strategic concept on external or internal security can only be wishful thinking left to the idle intellectuals. In case the answer is positive then it's relevant if we have intellectual inputs by way of reading material, literature which are conducive to such thinking and whether we have an army of thinkers to ignite the spark which could generate the requisite intellectual environment. The answer is definitely not very heartwarming and it is in this context the efforts of Dr Chauhan to author the books as varied as intelligence craft, war, internal subversive organisations/ cults and biological weapons, and should be viewed as welcome relief, in filling the intellectual vacuum.

Let us first see as to what is meant by the strategic military thinking. It is very simple to state. In layman's term it is the ability of a nation's political, military or intellectual component, may be all put together, to anticipate the action plan of our enemy or adversary which could jeopardize the internal as well as external security of our nation. In reality, it is not only an anticipation of enemy's game plan but what efforts we are making or have made to pre-empt such evil designs. Military strategy can best succeed not by merely sending a soldier with arms and ammunition but it can be fruitful only when political wisdom, the will of the patriotic citizens and expert knowledge available to the leadership from the intellectuals inputs by way of the creative literature on the subject, all amalgamated as one.

In geo-political context, strategic thinking on the issue of a nation's integrity and sovereignty is not a wishful thinking or a flight of fantasy. Sanctity of geographical boundaries is always vulnerable to evil designs of political strategy of an adversary or enemy. To achieve the strategical goals, sound planning by way of infrastructure, connectivity with every nook and corner of the nation, military preparedness and taking the citizens on loop for fulfillments of the goals are pre-requisites. Unfortunately, all these factors were never considered in the past in right earnest and the nation had to be suffer the ignominy of utter humiliation in the short-war of 1962 against China. The intelligence inputs were constantly ignored and expert advice from the military was always ridiculed by our Defence Minister in those days who once contemptuously commented "since when have the army generals have started thinking."

A very interesting but demoralising incident was narrated to us by the father of Sapna Pathania, who is co-author of this book. While serving in the army, he was sent on deputation in 1966 to Assam Rifles and was appointed as post commander of the post HURI in Subanshri division of N.E.F.A. (now Arunachal Pradesh). The post comprised of just over 200 men with an area of respansibility of depending 2500 sq. kilometers, along the MacMohan Line. The post was accessible by a strenuous walk of 15 days by foot crosing main Himalayan mountain ranges from the nearest road head in Assam. One fine morning, he was informed by the security guards that the post was seized by the tribals of the Taxing region of the division. The leader of the gang made himself comfortable in the office chair of the post commander. Some sat on the office table and few on the floors. They looked quite menacing with DHOW (a sword like weapon) hanging from their waist. This weapon is something akin to their part of body which is so sharp that they can cut a huge tree into pieces in a matter of few hours. The tribal chief unlike the other tribes of the area had Aryan features and never looked like the inhabitants of the area. So to the utter surprise of the post commander they had a very congenial mental disposition and had come to the post only to take permission to go to China for their shopping. The post commander had no authority to grant them such permission and therefore rightly persuaded them to go to cities in plains of Assam which they refused point blank on the grounds as to why they should walk on foot for fifteen days to go to Indian cities when they could achieve their goal just by walking for three days by going to China. The Mc-Mohan Line had no sanctity for them whatsoever. They found infrastructure placed on Chinese side more to their liking. No one knows what happened thereafter and no one was keen to know either. What surprised the post commander more than their defiance were their bodily features. He was later told by his knowledgeable interpreters that they were the remnants' of the Alexander's army who had made the north-east their abode centuries back to conceal themselves from the utter annihilation the rising Magadha empire. We have just witnessed in the foregoing paragraphs the utter neglect of the strategic inputs from the field commanders. The other factors which have surfaced now cannot be ignored altogether could these are the mutual psychological disconnect amongst our own citizens. Unfortunately we continue to harbour such prejudices even today. To us this appears to be the genesis of the Mao-insurgency in the states of Andhra, Maharashtra, Jharkhand, West Bengal and Chhatisgarh. Unless and until we bridge the gap of psychological disconnect by the intellectual inputs we shall continue to witness such tendencies which could continue to pose a serious threat to our internal security. We do not deny there are other numerous factor which are known to everyone and do not merit repetition. We all are aware but too arrogant to admit and thus our vision of national security strategy gets blurred.

With the passage of time of our history, we appear to have jettisoned the concept of the strategic thinking on matters which are of vital concern to our national security and integrity. We are quite contended that the international boundaries down on the map in the form of Mc Mohan Line in the eastern sector and Durand Line in the western front are a natural guarantee to our sovereignty. We must be grateful for the vision of our ancestors but nothing substantial was done to consolidate their vision. Although there have been no invasions from the western sector in modern history the conventional strategy has been replaced by economic war by way of quantum of smuggling of narcotics into our country which is an equally potent threat and capable of destabilising our socio cultural and political structure.

We are living in an environment of in-tellectual vacuum. All our intellectual activities are utility-based which may provide relief to us from the day-to-day rigours of the life but there is nothing for the posterity to emulate. We do not know as to what is the status of achievements in the literary domain in other languages but in the field of Hindi Literature works of status of "KAMAYANI" by Jai Shankar Prasad and "ANDHAYUG" by Dr Dharamvir Bharti have not seen the light of the day. So is the case in the field of novels, short stories or criticism, it may appear to be a very tall claim but the fact that the creative outputs of old stalwarts continue to dominate the curriculum of university education as nothing new is available for addition. Infact, out of the box thinking instead of being applauded is either ridiculed or ignored altogether.

At this juncture we are tempted to share an information, although we cannot vouch for its factual authenticity nevertheless it has a very purposeful message for all of us even today. It was sometimes in late fifty's that one brigadier who was posted in the general staff of the corps headquarters based at Tejpur was visiting the forward posts in his area of responsibility in the eastern sector. As he had nothing to do much during his visit he visualised a hypothetical scenario as to how the Chinese will attack us in a future war although it was blasphemous even to think on such a probability. In armed forces such hypothetical conjunctures are called "Appreciation" and taught to the cadets of any military academy at the very entry point of the career itself. The appreciation paper was forwarded to Prime Minister Office out of sheer curiosity. Needless to say the paper was torn and thrown in the dustbin. At a later point of time when the real Chinese attack developed, it was precisely on the same lines as hypothetically appreciated by the said officer in his appreciation paper. Nehru, the then Prime Minister who had thrown the paper as rubbish recollected each line of it and look at the magnanimity of his character that he not only met the said officer but apologised for not passing his view point. Sadly valuable time was post prime-facie, it may appear quite irrelevant and questions may be asked to us to as to why we are addressing the dynamics of the military strategy, in a biography of a police officer who has nothing to do with military matters. Very few realise that in the event of war, it is the civil administration who has to rise to the occasion, to preserve and protect the fort of the governance, to provide relief to the suffering millions for years to come even after a war is over. They can perform their functions best when they are familiar with the dynamics of the military strategy which has crucial beaming on internal security.

Dr Chauhan could have choosen an easier path for himself by confining himself to creative fields which were in line with his own academic background but he chose a more challenging field to author books on matters relating to intelligence craft, terrorist organisations. War in the middle east and biological war fore knowledge of which is of paramount interest to any military strategician, administrator or a political thinker. It is a matter of great satisfaction that he has acquitted himself exceedingly well in his chosen field and his contribution has not gone unnoticed in the world community and he is one of the speakers in the world on the subject of the bio-terrorism. He has definitely given the required impetus to the strategic culture as we shall discover it for ourselves when we undertake an effort to understand his creative written works. He has definitely succeeded in reviving the immense interest in military strategic thinking and culture in our intellectual community which is very vital to our internal security.

# Chapter XI

# Understanding Multi-Dimensional Creative Works of Dr Chauhan-An Introduction

There is a famous saying attributed to Earnest Hemingway that "one must write when drunk and edit when sober." We do not know how far it can be true but can safely assume that he must have said so jokingly as the celebrated novelist and noble laureate was fully aware that to became an author was a very serious business. In any case, Dr Chauhan defers and is credited with penning down multi-dimensional creative works as varied as state craft, military craft and matters relating to pure science and technology. This inspite of the fact that he chose to undertake these projects when he was extremely busy to deal with the commitments enjoined upon him by his professional calling in the Police Force with rare zeal, enthusiasm and host of inconveniences. He has succeeded to enrich our understanding relating to sovereignty and integrity of our country. His published works which have came to our notice are:-

(i) War on Iraq
(ii) Al-Qaeda
(iii) Inside CIA- Lessons in Intelligence
(iv) Biological weapons

(v) The Right to Information Act-2005 along with the Punjab Right to Information Rules-2005 (Translated in Punjabi).

All the above books have been published by APH Publishing Corporation, the first two in the year, 2003 and the last two in the year, 2004. The translation work has however been published by Bright Law House, Delhi.

As biographers, we would not attempt any critical scrutiny into his works because of lack of our orientation on the subjects and will leave it to the professionals in the field. We shall however still make a genuine effort to go into his intents rather than contents and also analyse the psychological dynamics which have motivated him to undertake such an arduous task.

As we made a passing reference in earlier chapters, it is quite interesting to note as to why contrary to his academic background, training and professional calling, he did not go after the stereotype subjects which would have made his job much easier. The answer fortunately is too visible to go unnoticed. To us it appears that Dr Chauhan has a keen sense of history and deliberately chooses the subjects relating to war, state craft and latest developments in the field of biological weapons which have very crucial bearing on our internal as well as external security.

It is a historical fact that foreign invasions into India which virtually changed the historical landscapes of our country were launched by the leaders in foreign lands thousands of miles away from us in the western parts of the Indian sub-continents Saka, Huns, and Kushans belonged to the distant lands. So was Babur, a tribal chief of Central Asia, who by any standards was not a military campaigner of repute but succeeded in defeating Indian kings and thus he succeeded in establishing a Mughal dynasty in India. It may be recalled that Babur had made three attempts to capture Samarkand in Central Asia to establish his kingdom but failed miserably each time. He had no choice but to turn east towards Afghanistan, where he did have some success which cannot be attributed to his military skills. Fortunately for him the Afghani's were themselves divided sharply fighting for supremacy amongst themselves. Although he succeeded in suppressing them militarily he could never subjugate them effectively and the Afghanis were a constant threat to his authority. Babur found the climate too hot for his own survival. His inclinations towards the life of comfort and luxury and his love for wines added further to his discomfort. He had no choice but look further East and the result was emergence of the Mughal dynasty which virtually ruled India roughly three centuries. The entry of Turkish war mercenaries is rather more interesting. They entered the court of Mughal emperor Jehangir in the disguise of men of letters and in due course succeeded in infiltrating combatant men in India. They did not go overboard with their initial success, as to challenge the Mughal authority would have been unpragmatic and therefore they assumed the role of friend and volunteered to rescue son of Aurangzeb whose son was taken as a captive in the fort of Bijapore by the Marathas. All the logistic lines to Mughal army were cut off and Aurangzeb was facing a certain defeat. The Turkish mercenaries bailed out Aurangzeb and for which they were suitably rewarded. The establishment of the Nizam dynasty is central India was the direct consequence of the declining Mughal supremacy.

No wonder owing to this historical backdrop, the Middle East becomes of vital interest to Dr Chauhan which may have motivated him to start his intellectual journey by authoring a book "War on Iraq". War on Iraq has a potential threat to our own security and its consequential fall outs may have been too threating to our internal security. A little effort to read between the lines in his book will reveal us his real intentions and contours of his psychological dynamics to understand war on Iraq. To understand the dynamics of his mind-set we intend to devote a chapter each to his published works which follows hereafter.

# Chapter XII

# War on Iraq - Its Relevance - Understanding Psychological Dynamics of Author

To understand the scenario in Iraq let us see its geographical location and ethnic composition. The Republic of Iraq has its boundaries with Turkey, Iran, Saudi Arabia, Jordan and Syria. About sixty per cent consists of Shia schism and approximately twenty per cent are Sunnies Muslims and Kurds. The rest constituting a mix of Armenians, Christians, Yazidis and Assyrians etc. its strategic geographical location and multi-ethnic composition allows the unique benefit to influence the political thought not only in the reason but beyond. Iraq therefore, secretly harboured the concept of global domination by bringing into the Islamic fold the infidels, a tag attached to the non-Muslim nations.

It is customary for any author of books on war to summarise the outcome of the war, highlighting the wisdom and folly in equal measure. Dr Chauhan deliberately skips this exercise since he does not want to impose his ideas on the intelligent readers. Nonetheless he has marshalled the valuable facts which are store house of very useful inputs. In a way the information made available to us by way of consequences of the war by itself sufficiently reveals the analysis of the war.

In any case, the conclusion drawn by him would have become irrelevant in the latest political developments in the region. It is said that the history repeats itself but it chooses its own time to repeat which cannot be easily forecast or anticipated. One thing is becoming very crystal clear that policy of shoot and scoot by the American has not yielded any desired results which was their prime motive to intervene militarily and within a span of a decade. The armed uprising of the Sunni fundamentalist has again driven to the state to the point of uncertainty and possible lapse of the existing political model.

Dr Chauhan through his painstaking efforts and valuable research has marshalled very useful information on Iraqi's weapons of mass-destruction, chemical and biological weapons besides nuclear capabilities as these existed on the ground before the war on Iraq. The information is further corroborated by the fact that Saddam Hussain, the then dictator of Iraq never hesitated to use these chemical weapons against his own Kurd tribes. There is no reason to infer that he would have abstained from using these weapons against his international adversaries. In the light of this clinching evidence, there is sufficient justification for declaring war on Iraq on March, 19th in the year 2003 by the NATO forces lead by the United States which resulted in fall of Saddam and installation of democratic regime.

The pertinent question which now emerges is as to what is the relevance of Dr Chauhan's efforts to author a book on war in Iraq in the changed scenario. In our opinion notwithstanding the completion of successful military campaign, some splinter groups of fundamentalists/*jehadies* go underground and re-appear at an opportune time which unfortunately we are witnessing now. The second but more important question which haunts us now is that bombs cannot subdue fanaticism however disruptive and harmful and it is possible only at intellectual level to root out the misplaced thinking by resorting to educational and re-consistory approaches. The Sunnies insurgency against the rulers is resulting into killing of innocents civilians and distruction of property.

By destroying legitimate rule, the Sunni insurgents are taking over the administrative control, as a result of their actions a civil war like situation has been created, how it is going to unfold is a big puzzle. The questions also arise as to who are providing these insurgents the logistic support, arms and ammunition to achieve their goals. The possibility of functionaries in the current establishment cannot be ruled out altogether as they may be helping the insurgents, loyalty is a precious commodity in the Iraqis political system and even Saddam Hussain was plagued by the genetic negative thinking. It is interesting to note that Uday, the son of Saddam Hussein, who founded the organisation Fidayeen Saddam (Saddam's men of sacrifice) was removed from the command because in few cases he exhibited the tendencies of by-passing his father without his knowledge or concurrence. The strength of this force was equivalent to the strength of three infantry divisions (roughly 60000) who were recruited from the area loyal to Saddam and were not a part of any chain of command of the Iraqi army. Saddam's own elite bodyguard component called special security service was ruthless against any dissent.

The most frustrating part of the developing scenario is that no one knows for certain as to whom the authority vests leading the insurgency. The hesitation of the United States to intervene is definitely borne out of owing to uncertainty. It is definitely difficult to deal with a bunch of sciziophernic individuals as their experience of dealing with only one Saddam was difficult to be forgotten.

The pertinent question is as to in what way the war on Iraq authored by Dr Chauhan is helpful to us in understanding the gravity of changing and fluid political scenario. The relevance of the Iraq war or subsequent uprisings shall ever remain of immense value to us as it has direct bearing on our economic, social and security environment.

Any war or war like scenario in the Middle East has very serious fall out for the Indian economy. We are already reaching under the inflation which is bound to get aggravated further. As we know we are heavily dependent on oil imports, from the region to augment our energy resources the shortfall in energy output with have adverse effect on production. Though our oil imports are based on long-term contracts but these are subject to constant periodical review. Further, the contracts loose their sanctity because oil supplies can either be stopped altogether or curtailed drastically. The scenario on internal security is equally demoralising as highly indoctrinated *jihadi* groups are likely to infiltrate into our country causing serious concerns to our internal security set-up. After all we should not forget that Ahl-E-Hadees a *jihadi* organisation supported by Saudi Arbia is responsible for genocide of the Shia Muslims in Pakistan. Leave alone the Middle East, even Egypt is affected by an identical organisation called "Muslim Brotherhood" so is the demoralising scenario in Algeria and Yemen. These organisations have no respect for political boundaries of a nation and can switch over to any geographical area. Militants of Lashkar-e-Toiba and head of Jamat-Ud-Dawa, Hafiz Saeed, openly extort the militants to spread their tentacles to Kashmir in India and further upto Mynmar. In any case the outcome of the current political developments in Iraq are definitely grave and call for effective counter-measures to contain the menace.

We can never build a castle on earth without having a solid foundation. To have an effective shield against destabilising forces to our political, social, economic and internal security environment we must have a sound knowledge of history of the region to develop a vision to safeguard against such destabilising forces.

It is said that knowledge is power and Dr Chauhan enriches our understanding to equip ourself against unforeseen contingencies arising out of adventures of the Jihadi organisations around us. Our spiritual texts to enhance the quality of life motivate us saying "know thyself but it is equality important to have a re-look on alternative slogans as well and it could rightly be "know thy neighbours."

# Chapter XIII

# The Al Qaeda Threat- A Never Ending Threat-Understanding Psychological Dynamics of Author

The next book, authored by Dr Chauhan which aroused our curiosity is titled *"The Al-Qaeda Threat"* and we had enthusiastically taken it out from, our book shelf. We know that it would not be a pleasant reading as the title of the book suggested. However, we were quite certain that it would provide us with the gory details besides enable us in understanding a terrorist organisation and their *jihadi* mind set which has shaken the civilised world like a storm.

India is one of the five countries in the world which are most affected by the onslaught of the terrorism. The terrorism essentially results in colossal loss of life of security personnel, misguided youths and other innocent citizens. Further, it puts our meager financial resources and tax-payee hard earned money to sheer waste in containing such tendencies. The pace of developmental activities cannot undertake in conflict zones affected by the terrorism.

The Al-Qaeda terrorist organisation ows its origin to an organisation "Mehtab of Khindamat (the service office)" which had its offices in various part of the world. From 1989, onwards the group called itself "Al-Qaeda". In 1996, the group re-located itself in Afghanistan from Sudan where it was originally located and the leadership was handed over to Osama-bin-Laden. Its objective were to:-

1. Establishing the rule of god on the earth.
2. Attaining the martyrdom in the name of god.
3. Purifying the ranks of Islam from the elements of depravity.

To achieve their objective it is but essential that besides religious indoctrination they concentrate more and more on the training of Jihadis to ensure success of their goals. It is not surprising that their training capsule is modelled on the training manual of any modern military force of the world. They not only carry out the basic courses but advance courses as well. The encyclopaedia of Afghan Jihad curtains over 7000 pages in Arabic language which was produced by their training department. The important chapters are:-

(i) Explosives
(ii) Manufacturing and assembly
(iii) Killing from close range
(iv) Hand guns
(v) Security and intelligence
(vi) Tactics
(vii) Bombs and landmine
(viii) Tanks
(ix) First aid
(x) Topography and distance movement
(xi) Manual on how to make chemical and biological weapons.

Dr Chauhan has rendered yeomen's service by preferring to choose a subject which threatens international peace and stability, India included. He has brought out systematically, the structure selection of Jihadi, their training and regimentation which enables them to challenge even the militarily most powerful nations in the world today.

The Al-Qaeda is an umbrella organisation which now promotes other terrorist groups across the world. The only common thing among themselves being that they stand for the purity of the Islamic ideology which according to them has been corrupted by the infidels namely, those who do not believe in Islamic ideology. The aims of this organisation can roughly be summarised as under :-

(i) To promote the Islamic struggle and entity

(ii) To throw the corrupt Islamic regimes influenced by the western influence

(iii) To undertake specific mission to spread terror

(iv) To create financial networks globally to achieve financial independence.

To appreciate their aims and objectives better, let us go into their structural compensation, selection, training and regimentation regime of the terrorist organisation.

The Al-Qaeda organisation consists of the main members, which consisted of founding members along-with their die-hard supporters to begin with and is called the core group. They are the ideologues of the organisation. Although the organisation is based in Afghanistan it is very difficult to identify their exact location as they prefer safe hideouts for themselves and also keep on moving their headquarters to escape detection. It is, therefore very difficult to state with any degree of certainty as to where they are at a given time. Osama-bin-Laden (since eliminated) in a daring operation undertaken by US Seal Commandos was their head and the other member consisted of AYMAN-Al-Zawahiri who was earlier head of a Egyptian Islamic group Al-Jehad. He, not only belonged to an illustrious political family of the Egypt but himself was a leading surgeon by training. Mohammed Atef, another Egyptian, was responsible for military planning of the organisation. He is an ex-police officer and unconfirmed reports suggest that he has since been killed in air strike by the United States. The structural group is headed by Abu Zabaydah, Saudi-national and is responsible for recruitment and training of the jihadis. Jahir Yulashev is an Uzbeck national and trains jihadi fighters. Amir Khattak is a Saudi national, Khadaffy Janjlani is a Philippine and D Jamel Beghal an Algerian, Sayakh Saeed is the finance chief. The persons of this structural group simultaneously also head smaller terrorist organisation which are engaged in terrorist activities under Al-Qaeda guidance and financial help. Though all these functionaries hail from Islamic countries their nationalities give it an identity which is global and therefore more deadly. It has a well-oiled machinery of support groups and operations cells. The careful reading of Al-Qaeda threat by Dr Chauhan reveals very interesting facts about the recruitment, training and indoctrination of jihadis which Directorates of training of any modern military machines may try to emulate.

Let us see the nomenclature of the organisation Al-Qaeda means "the base" which apparently is a misnomer and quite misleading as it reveals nothing about its identity and goals which is the guiding force of their existence. Although to begin with, its aim was to support war efforts against the Soviets in Afghanistan and surprisingly they even enjoyed the patronage of the United States. But after the withdrawal of the Soviets it grew as a monster and trained jihadi fighters, spread its tentacles to Egypt, Algeria and Saudi Arabia and focused its attention against the United States and allies who were considered infidels and were constantly engaged in armed intervention against the Islamic countries. In due course, the Al-Qaeda grew as an international militant organisation to reckon with and appropriated the role of a trainer of local jihadi groups in different countries to promote islam and also provided them with financial help.

As the organisation grew in stature and its lethal capabilities increased correspondingly they raised the bench mark to recruit the members of the jihadi groups to advance their ideology. These pre-requisites are listed below:-

(i) The member of the organisation should be a Muslim
(ii) He should have the commitment to the organisation ideology
(iii) Maturity
(iv) Sacrifice
(v) Listening to leadership and obedience
(vi) Temperament of keeping secrets and conceding information
(vii) Free of illness
(viii) Patience
(ix) Tranquility and unflappability
(x) Intelligence and insight
(xi) Truthfulness
(xii) Ability to observe and analyse
(xiii) Ability to change positions and conceal one-self

Needless to say all these characteristics are mandatory prerequisites before being admitted into the fold of the Al-Qaeda. It must be very onerous task of the psycho-analytical team of the organisation assigned the task of recruitment. It also speaks volumes of the skills of the recruiting team to identify these traits in an individual. The persons so recruited are called agents although they are integral part of fighting force. The fact that the persons recruited were in thousands of numbers from different nationalities, it is really commendable the way they have gone about their job. Just imagine the finished product of the raw material in the form of new recruits after they have undergone requisite training and indoctrination in terrorist ideology. It is a foregone conclusion that any terrorist organisation can hardly match the military might of a state. It is infact their tactics, stealth and tricks of deception which make them deadly and more effective in comparison with superior forces because conventional forces engaged to contain them proceed in a copy book fashion. They have careful selection of their target which could be a strategic building, important establishments, radio and television stations, bridges and most important the selection of personalities to be eliminated. Apparently they do not require a very large force to accomplish these tasks. A question therefore arises as to what is their intention to have a large force of the vast human resources trained as Jihadis notwithstanding their unconventional tactics they do not leave anything to chance. In case state machinery initiates an all out offensive against them, the residual elements of these organisation always try to slip away and re-organise again to achieve their goal. In our view even the state machinery should invent new methodology to meet the challenges. The United States has certainly innovated some tactics like 'Smoke them Out" before any military action.

The media reports indicate that the Pakistan has launched operation ZARBE AZB (the sharp cut) against Tahreek-I-Taliban Pakistan (TTP) bases in Waziristan and a full corps strength (roughly 60000 thousand troops) using tanks, artillery and air-force are engaged to annihilate the terrorist bases. The bases they may destroy but what about the jihadi who were operating from such bases. In the face of such superior strength and fire power they are bound to escape mixing alongwith the large exodus of the civilian population to safety in Afghanistan and would continue to pose problems not only to Pakistan but more to India. This TTP is noting but Al-Qaeda in new avtar (incarnation) and may pose grave threat to our own internal security in future.

The targets selected by the Al-Qaeda are pre-determined and are chosen after careful thought to have maximum demoralising effect. Thus, these targets require specific type of expertise for successful executions. The targets selected in distant lands also require the local Jihadi groups support. The selection of Jihadis is therefore a very complicated and careful exercise. The persons so selected are called agents have to pass through numerous stages to test their capabilities and these are:-

(i) *Finding the agent-* a careful scrutiny is done to verify the financial condition, family status, his career profile, his strength and weaknesses are carefully examined to verify the suitability of the agent.

(ii) *Evaluation of the agent-* the agent is part of constant secret surveillance to evaluate his loyalty and competence.

(iii) *Approaching the agent-* the process is carried out in utmost secrecy to ensure that the plan is not compromised.

(iv) *Testing the integrity of the agent-* integrity is put to severe test by offering false inducements.

(v) *Training of the agent-* after an agent has successfully crossed the preceding hurdles he undergoes specific type of training essential for execution of the task.

Success of any terrorist operation depends on ensuring that no information howsoever trivial it may seem comes to notice of the hawk eyes of the intelligence agencies of the nation being targeted. Their own counter-intelligence system is therefore highly sophisticated and elaborate that they even have their own cryptographic codes. Their counter intelligence system is so effective that intelligence agencies of their adversaries are uncertain as to on whom the responsibility of leadership of Al-Qaeda has fallen after elimination of Osama-bin-Laden.

Dr Chauhan has brought meticulously the details of their methodology. Inspite of efforts much is needed to learn about their weapons of mass destruction, although Dr Chauhan has made the efforts to list these weapons in the appendix to the book.

A very vital question may be asked as to what is the utility of Dr Chauhan's efforts in the context of our own internal and external security. We would like to pose the counter-question to recollect as to how can we easily forget the advance military forces disguised as Kabailies infiltrators in the state of Jammu & Kashmir in the year 1947-48 and occupation of strategic Kargil heights by so called shepherds in the year, 1998. Were these elements really Kabailies (shepherded) or shepherds as had been claimed by our neighbour. The answer is definitely no, since no disorganised groups can fight a pitched battle with regular security forces. These were definitely state-sponsored attempt to either annex our territory or pose serious challenges to our national security. No one can really forecast as to what shall be the new incarnation of Al-Qaeda to meet their India specific terror operations. The problem assuming much more significance, as we are currently facing problem of Mao insurgency covering roughly two-third districts of India in the State of Chhattishgarh, Jharkhand, Andhra, Maharashtra and few districts of West Bengal. We shall never forget that Al-Qaeda is an umbrella terror organisation which supports local jihadi operations in roughly sixty countries of the world. We can ill afford to presume that Al-Qaeda will have no role to play in the evil designs of militant organisation operating in India. The Mao insurgents roughly use the same tactics as those practiced by the Al-Qaeda and needs to be studied in detail.

Even otherwise, let us put it very frankly if the media reports are to be believed that Al-Qaeda is actively planning to liberate Kashmir and a huge contingents of Jihadi have already left Afghanistan. To substantiate their propaganda they have even released a video tape of their semester designs.

We know for certain that all militant activities in state of J&K are fuelled and fanned by Inter Services Intelligence (ISI) of our western neighbouring country and whenever their agents are captured they wash off their hands by saying that they have no role whatsoever and have coined a new word in political jargon on calling them non-state actors and pretend that they have no control over them. But the fact that these infiltrators are heavily armed with sophisticated weapons, carry enough currency and even dry fruits to survive till they link-up with their sleeping modules in India. We hope that they will remember the speech delivered by Hillary Clinton in a seminar when she declared that you cannot have snakes in your backyard under the presumption that these will bite only your neighbours.

Dr Chauhan has meticulously brought out all the aspects and sinister designs of Al-Qaeda organisation and its adverse impact on the liberal democrate institution across the world including India. If Dr Chauhan has withheld any information, we understand his limitations as, he is an uniformed service officer and pointing out the needle of suspicion in unequivocal terms may hamper our genuine efforts for peace with the neighbour. A simple question we ourselves would like to ask those who advance the alibi of the non-state actors as to who provided the safe haven to Osama-bin-Laden adjacent to a very heavily guarded national military academy. He, too, according to their own definition was a non-state actor. No wonder our neighbour assumed a stony silence when the seal commandoes of the US Army picked up and killed him in daring helicopter operation. The history shall bring but the facts sooner than expected by the utter embarrassment of our western neighbour at some point of time in future.

# Chapter XIV

# "Inside CIA- Lessons in Intelligence" An Insight into Intelligence Culture - Understanding Psychological Dynamics of Author

As the title of this chapter suggests the third book authored by Dr Chauhan which we have taken for our scrutiny is a monumental effort by him to venture into a virgin subject which by and large is kept well concealed from the public domain. We have no clue with regard to the organisation functions and modus operandi of this segment of any sovereign state and rightly so since any intelligence organisation is primarily responsible to provide safeguards against the dangers to our national security. Since its activities are essentially covert we know hardly any thing about their role. Thus, we have not even rudimentary, knowledge of our own intelligence outfits leave alone of any other foreign country.

The scenario in the United States of America is however slightly different. Whatever may be the truth at least they make us to believe so. The change in public perception about intelligence agencies whatever its creditability may be, started surfacing when Edward J. Epstein published a number of articles on the subject. It contained so much information that he was suspected of having a role in the intelligence agency which in actuality was not true. In fact David Martin published a book in 1980 titled "*Wilderness of Mirrors*" which is considered a classic in literature relating to intelligence. Even he was suspected to have access to many CIA retirees. Such trends were also noticed when by the end of 1980, a British authors also started criticising British internal security agency (MI5) and also external secret intelligence service known as MI6.

We have no intention to suggest that the public participation in the intelligence matter is desirable for the very simple reason that in the long run such liberalisation may render any intelligence organisation totally ineffective as well as redundant.

Our epic literature like Ramayana, clearly suggests that but for the superior intelligence systems Ram may have not succeeded to annihilate evil forces of Ravana. The master stroke of Ram was to grant asylum to Vibhishan to whom monkey forces were hell bent upon to kill. The utility of Vibhishan in the final outcome of war is well known and needs no recapitulation. Similar strategy is also in full manifestation when the art of deception and mis-information were effectively employed by Krishna in the Mahabharata War.

It was, however, Chanakya during the Murya period of our recorded history who gave a sound direction to the intelligence craft. It is no more a secret that he encouraged the culture by licensing drinking joints which were very vital source of intelligence gathering. He even liberally employed women, who were called Vish Kanyas (Poison Girls) in the intelligence operations which still finds its echo even today in the form of a clandestine operation which in our modern terminology is called "Honey Trap" and its deadly consequences. It shall be appropriate to share a true incident which was narrated to us by a seasoned intelligence officer which brings out the deadly consequences of "honey trap". There was a simple housewife whose husband was serving in an intelligence organisation. She had a very disturbed family life because her husband used to remain absent for days together with an alibi that he was engaged in some secret operations. She believed it to be true nevertheless requested a politically influential person to put a kind word to the concerned authorities that her husband's dedication to duty should not be exploited so as to effect his family life. The intelligence organisation where her husband was serving launched a discreet surveillance on him and to their utter surprise they found the officer in a hotel with a lady who was on the look out list of the Interpol organisation as she was an agent of a notorious outfit engaged in subversive activities. The lady in question was ostensibly on a cover job as an air hostess by using false passport. The matter was too serious for the image of the government and therefore the case was hushed up and the delinquent officer was dispatched to some inhospitable corner of India where he languished for a number of years.

The pertinent question which obviously is of utmost importance to our national security is as to what is this business called the intelligence. According to our perception, any knowledge is power and thus secret knowledge is a secret power. The secret knowledge therefore is an effective shield to safeguard our national interests against economic, social, political and cultural invasion against the evil designs of our adversaries. We however would prepare to quote more acceptable definitions of intelligence as cited in the book "*Inside Cia*" Walter Laqeur the author of "A world of secrets:- the uses and limits of intelligence is of the view that all attempts to develop ambitious, theories of intelligence have failed. But in the event of absence of an acceptable definition we would be at a loss to understand the aims and purpose of intelligence. The other definition quoted in the book read as under:-

"Intelligence deals with all the things which should be known in advance of initiating a course of action."

One high ranking official who was the true student of the intelligence craft defines it "Intelligence is the knowledge and ideally fore knowledge sought by nations in response to the external threats and to protect their vital interests specially the well being of their own people."

Council of foreign relations commissioned the study by the American establishment defined it as "Intelligence is information not publicly available or analysis based on such information that has been prepared for policy-makers or other actors inside the government."

All these definitions suffer from the bias that for too much emphasis to laid on the word information. Fortunately, we get a satisfactory answer to our query as National Intelligence Council defines it as "Intelligence is the process by which specific type of information, important to national security are requested, collected, analysed and provided to the policy-makers, the product that process, safeguarding of these processes and this information by counter-intelligence activities and the carrying out of operation as required by the lawful authorities" on the force of it, it may appear too lengthy but it definitely addresses our ignorance to comprehend the exact import of the word intelligence. It underlines the basic difference between information and intelligence because any information which cannot be corroborated is always of zero value.

We tried to ascertain as to what exactly is the organisational set up, order of hierarchy and chain of command in the American Central Intelligence Agency to understand its functions but drew a blank. We, however, do find a brief description relating to vision, mission, core beliefs and values of the agency, however, to us it appears to be charter of duties which are elucidated in the book as under:-

(A) Mission—"To be the key stone of the intelligence community that is pre-eminent in the world known for both the high quality of our work and the excellence of our people. We support the President, National Security Council and all those who make and execute US National Security Policy by –

- Providing accurate evidence based on comprehensive and timely foreign intelligence related to national security and conducting counter Intelligence activities, special activities and other functions related to foreign intelligence and national security as directed by the President.
- Our core beliefs and values.

**What we stand for**

- Intelligence that of substantial value to the management of crises, the conduct of war and development of policy.
- Objectively in the substance of intelligence, a deep commitment to the customer in its form and timing.
- How Do We Work.
- Personal and organisational integrity.
- Team work throughout the agency and intelligence community.
- Total participation of an excellent and diverse work force.
- Innovating and taking risks to get the job done.
- Adopting to both, a changing world environment and evolving customers' needs.
- Accepting accountability to our actions.
- Continuous in all that we do.

A careful study of their mission and methodology it appears that it conveys everything at the same time nothing as well. It all depends on the skill of the interpreter to get the real facts viz. they can do anything although they do not reveal an inch of their agenda and modus operandi but that is the business we call intelligence how do they achieve their goal?

We find answer to this puzzle which the book lists as fifteen axioms for intelligence analysers. These make interesting reading and are reproduced without any change. The interpretation of the axioms has been left to the intelligent readers. These axioms are reproduced as under:-

1. Always be willing to listen to alternative or other point of view but stand your ground if there are reasons to believe.
2. Be aggressive and do not fear being wrong.
3. Better to be mistaken than be wrong.
4. Avoid mirror imaging i.e. projecting yourself through process on some one at all costs.
5. Intelligence is of no value if it is not disseminated.
6. Co-ordination is necessary but do not settle for the least common denominator or consenters to valuable but such shared assumptions may not be correct.
7. When everyone agrees on an issue something probably is wrong.
8. The consumer does not care how much you know. Just tell him what is important.
9. Form is never more important than substance.
10. Aggressively persue collection of information you need.
11. Do not take editing process too seriously.
12. Know your community counterparts and talk to them frequently.
13. Never let your career take precedence over your job.
14. Being an intelligence analyst is not a popularity contest.
15. Do not take your job on yourself too seriously i.e. the fate of the world does not rests on your shoulders. There will always be more than there is time to do. Do not become a work alcoholic. Take care of yourself and family.

The efforts in collection of information and its conversion into an actionable intelligence will be totally nullified if we fail to deny the information about ourselves to our adversaries. It is equally to important to deny any information which may run counter to our own national interests when any nation grows in financial stability and develops a foolproof security apparatus around itself, it naturally generates jealousy and resentment in its rivals. It is, therefore, imperative that we deny any information to our adversaries which may boost their effects on our parts are called counter-intelligence operations and are as important and vital as the collection of intelligence. Thus, counter-intelligence in another side of the coin of the intelligence craft.

The books *"Inside CIA"* by Dr Chauhan lists Ten Commandments of the counter-intelligence operations and is listed below. Once again we would refrain to endorse any explanatory notes to these commandments test we dilute their essence. These are:-

1. Be offensive.
2. Honour your professionals.
3. Own the street (read dominate).
4. Know your history.
5. Do not ignore analysis.
6. Do not be parochial.
7. Train your people.
8. Do not be shoved aside.
9. Do not stay too long.
10. Never give up.

As pointed earlier, the intelligence community is feared by their own citizens all over the world forgetting the fact that they are doing their job for security and safety of the nation. Even American call the CIA as a rouge elephant. We are certainly not so biased in our attitude but are definitely prejudiced against them in our assessment. Psduo-intellectuals think that these agencies are white elephants and can be dispensed with. There was a time in our own recent history when the political leadership contemplated abolishing our external intelligence agency called RAW. We are so biased against them that wherever they encounter any failure, we haul them for intelligence failure. Americans never say so and if such failure should occurs they simply say intelligence mistake. The task of the intelligence agencies to locate a needle in a dark tunnel and failures are bound to occur because they are exploring the unknown. We have to accept success or failure in the same stride.

It is not that the intelligence community is not aware of such erroneous perceptions. We witness a very passionate effort in the book "Inside CIA" to interpret and give a healthy perception to the two words which are primarily responsible for not understanding the dynamics of intelligence business. In chapter-XIII of the book titled integrity ethics and the CIA, the misgivings with regard to the interpretation of these are given new perception. In any language of the world meaning and interpretation of any word is always perceived in a specific context. If the context is removed, the meaning of the particular word also changes its contours. To understand the phenomenon more clearly let us re-visit the great epic Mahabharat, just before the war begins, Arjuna trembles in the battle field and is unable to focus on the job assigned to him. He believes the history shall always blame him for killing his own blood relatives which he considers unethical. To some extent logic may appear to be rational till Krishna convince him that the opponents are not his relatives but enemy and therefore there is nothing unethical to kill the enemy. Similarly, integrity also is given a new interpretation and it defines quote "Integrity also cover the idea that commitment to values is maintained even if it goes against one's self-interests to do so. In sense ethics similarly also implies doing the right thing even if it hurts unquote. We may question the operating culture of any organisation but we really do have no alternative to perform in any other way since that would jeopardize our own safety and security. The basic elements of these words are given entirely new meanings which are too convincing to be ignored and it also puts debate to rest. These are and we quote:-

(i) Belief in and awareness of the moral purpose of the agency mission.

(ii) Always speaking truth to power both within the agency and the policy maker we serve.

(iii) Doing your homework knowing when we have enough information to make a decision and explaining it with clarity and honestly what we cannot do or do not know.

(iv) Willingness to be held accountable to what we do, write and say.

(v) Taking calculated risk in obtaining and analysing information.

(vi) Responsible use of public money and honour knowing that we can always answer the question in affirmative.

(vii) Giving all employees an equal chance to achieve and be rewarded for excellence. Accepting and learning from failures as a means of continually improving who we are.

The CIA has a very positive work culture. They firmly believe "If you have not been wrong lately, you are not doing your job" and they believe and we quote "failures should be regarded opportunity for learning and growth rather than as curse for punishment and permanent stigmisation" unquote similarly on ethics they have crystal clear views. To them ethics is a evolving frame work of values that requires continued thought and attention. Nothing explaining better their standpoint on ethics which we learnt when few years back we were going though a book authored on Harry Truman the President of the United States when the second world war on its zenith and it was taking a heavy toll of the men and material around the globe, Harry Truman, the Vice President of the

United States was elevated to be the President of the United States owing to unavoidable circumstances. Even while Truman was Vice President, he was not aware of project of development of atomic bomb. See the irony of the unfolding of the events that he was to take the decision whether to use the atomic bomb in Japan. He however exercised the option to ascertain the public opinion on the issue a nationwide discreet survey which ruled in favour of the use of the atomic bomb fully knowing its unimaginable destructive capabilities. To survey indicated that the war of bomb about the possible loss of life and destruction of property would be much less comparable to the losses which would accrue if the war continued unabated end of which was never in subject. Our contention that the ethics and integrity are the terms which assume an altogether different meaning in a changed context.

The US has in-built mechanism which keeps the intelligence agency in control list it in appropriates the role of the decision-making authority. Firstly, besides periodical reports to the President it also submits its briefing to the Congress. It is however alleged that the briefing to the congress is filtered and it may be true as well but we should not forget that the briefer is always subject to cross-questioning by the Congress on its intelligence inputs. It is however different thing that the Congress is a mature body and they are aware of their limitations, more so on the subjects pertaining to national security. Yet another safeguard is that the agency has to submit the identical briefing to the President-elect in-spite of the fact that he had not taken the oath to be the President. It is done with a view that the incoming President is not handicapped for inadequate intelligence material when he takes over the responsibility. This also gives sharp insight to the next newly elected President into the affairs soon ofter taking over. The newly elect President also gets acquainted about the capabilities of the agency in which he has to depend heavily to have a realistic strategic view of the world affairs. It is interesting to learn that it was Harry Truman himself who introduced these practices which continue even today.

There is yet another surprising practice unlike any other nations India included is that the CIA can be headed by a non-career professional. But it has enough safeguards against any misuse of the authority. Although due care is taken to select the person at the time of appointment it is ensured that the charter of the agency remain apolitical. Further the inputs from the other intelligence agencies like Department of States, National Security Agency, Defense Intelligence Agency and Joint Chiefs of Staff act as effective watch dogs to check the credibility of the Agency. Even the think tank available with the President also ensure that the agency confines itself to furnish only the facts on intelligence related issues and do not across the red line by giving recommendations on police formulations which is an exclusive domain of the executive authority.

Dr Chauhan has rendered an invaluable service to the intelligence community by his methodical research efforts which we witness on the *"Inside CIA- Lessons in Intelligence."* The book is of immense value not only to the students of intelligence craft but also to those who are engaged in the craft. We however feel that a detailed commentary by the author in the shape of an explanatory preface would have been icing on the cake.

## Chapter XV

# "Biological Weapons"- A New Concept in Warfare-Understanding Psychological Dynamics of Author

In our persuit of appraisal of scholarly contribution of Dr Chauhan, the book which we have chosen is titled "Biological Weapons".

In chapter three of the book Dr Chauhan traces the history of biological warfare in the ancient period. In Biblican times, the evidence suggests the existence of biological weapons although these may have been in a very crude stage of development in comparison to the modern times as blood kumin, frogs, flies, boils, locusts, darkness and hails were extensively were not for behind and venom tipped arrows were used to kill.

In Indian epics too we do have evidence that the biological weapons were used to gain superiority over the enemy. In Ram Charit Manas a replica of original epic Ramayana by Valmiki there is sufficient evidence to suggest that the biological weapons were used by the army of Ravana against the forces of Ram in the battle field. We are tempted to quote from Ram Charit Manas which is written in Awadhi, a dialect of Hindi language by poet Tulsi Das. We shall however render a loose English translation of it for the benfit of English readers.

Let us see, what the scenario of the battle field was when Meghnad son of Ravana used these weapons against the army of Rama:-

नभ चढ़ि बरस विपुल अंगारा। महिते प्रगत होहि जलधारा।।
विष्ट, पूय, रुधिर कच हाडा। बरसइ कवहु उपल बहु छाड़ा।
वरिष धूरि कीन्हेसि अधियारा। सूझ न आपन हाथ पसारा।।

Loosely translated the above couplet would reveal that Meghnad rained fire and in certain cases illusion was created as if flood has taken place. He also rained pus, human excretion blood, bones and dust to create darkness that disoriented the enemy forces to the extent that they did not know as to what to do while fighting the enemy.

We cannot dismiss such scenario merely as a poetic imagination because fantasy has always some reality. By the time we come to the Mahabharta period of the epic which depicts the war between, Kaurvas and Pandavas the siblings of Kuru dynasty, it appear that the biological weapons had advanced and had acquired very lethal capabilities. Karna, a great warrior from the Kaurava forces had always cherished the ambition to kill Arjuna an equally talented army commander from the Pandava forces. Karna had a special missile reserved in stock to kill Arjuna. Krishna, the non-fighting strategician from the Pandava forces had no answer to Karna's missile. It was also a fact that if Arjuna was killed the battle was lost. Krishna therefore deployed Ghatotkach a tribal warlord who had reservoir of biological weapons and vast knowledge of biological warfare. In the daring night operation which forced Karna to use the missile intended to kill Arjuna. The greatest threat of defeat in the war was thus safely averted although Ghatotkach lost his life.

From the above two narratives, it is abundantly clear that there is sufficient evidence that destructive biological weapons were not only in existence but those were also used in the conduct of the war. It is a different thing that in the initial stages these may not have been so devastating and were used only as a war of attrition to disorient the enemy but with the passage of time these weapons had acquired the lethal capabilities by the time we came to the Mahabharata period roughly 3500 years before Christ. The modern day scholars may term our inferences as a figment of imagination but we would put the debate to rest by quoting AL Basham, the renowned scholar of Anthropology from Australia who said if you read the Indian epics as a history these appear to be poetry and if you read them as a poetry you shall find history in them.

So let us switch over as to what biological weapons are and what is their history. Dr Chauhan has very intelligently elucidated the growth as to how these weapons have evolved to cause a serious threat to the humanity and has become a global concern now.

In the documented history of India, the development and existence of biolgical weapons is clearly noticed during the period of Chanakya, the Prime Minister of Mauryan empire Chandra Gupta roughly 310 BC. In his immortal treatise "Arthshastra" Chanakya more known as the name of Kautilya in chapter one deals with certain concoctions to inflict injury on the enemy. Chapter two deals with preparation like changing skin colours, emitting light. Chapter three deals with aids which are very vital for success of stealth operations besides certain preparations which cause deadly diseases like gonorrea and a number of other mysterious disease. In medieval period, as recorded in the history, the Tartur army also used plague affected bodies in the enemy city to force them to surrender in the seize of Kaffa in 1346 AD. The manufacture of biological weapons has always been shrouded in secrecy. But as the intelligence community is aware that a secret remains no more a secret it comes to the knowledge of the two persons and it invariably comes to the knowledge of world sooner than imagined.

We once again want to reiterate that our effort of critical appraisal of the works authored by Dr Chauhan is not with a view to pass any judgement because the subject is highly scientific and technical and therefore leave it to the scholars of the concerned field. Our effort is motivated by some other considerations and we are primarily concerned with to understand how his intellectual curiosity has enabled him to lay before the world, the gravity of the dangers arising from biological weapons.

Let us see as to what is a biological weapon. Conventionally biological weapons are nothing but using germs against the humans. But the knowledge is now being used not only against humans but is being used as effective tool of destruction of crops and animals as well successful efforts have also been made which has resulted into manufacture of biological weapons capable of causing severe damage to the mental faculties of the human beings. A large number of viruses, bacteria, fungi have been used for manufacture of biological weapons. To name only a few these are:-

(i) Chikungunia virus.
(ii) Japanese encephalitis virus.
(iii) Yellow fever virus.
(iv) Small pox virus besides a number of bacteria and fungi.

The biological weapons have number of advantages over other weapons of mass destruction and few of these are:-

(i) Stealth weapon.
(ii) No smoking gun as in conventional weapons.
(iii) Cheapest.
(iv) Easy method of manufacture.
(v) Easy to conceal and camuflage.
(vi) Bacterial agents are cheap once the technology is mastered.

(vii) The weapons can be used against humans as well as against animal and crops.

(viii) Effective weapons against economic warfare.

(ix) Theoretically small quantities are required.

(x) Weapons of mass disruption.

(xi) Agents of weapon multiply when released.

The development of weapons is no more confined only to plagues, burns and other diseases like cholera, malaria, small pox etc. but genetic engineering biotechnology has opened new horizons in the destructive capacity of the biological weapons.

Dr Chauhan has listed over one hundred incidents in one of the chapters giving full details of the perpetrator, period and effects of biological weapons on those who were targeted. Unfortunately all these have been used not only by the states concerned but also non-state actors, a phenomenon we can hardly afford to ignore. The revelation that as to how Tamil Guerillas used biological agents against Sinhalese between 1983-87 and the followers of a little known man called Rajneesh used biological agents in the USA against the people who were against their cult. With the rise of the terrorist activities around the globe the unscrupulous use of the biological weapons by insurgents of the militant groups is a very frightening reality.

It is not that various states of the world community are free from guilt. As illustrated by the author in the biological warfare in a chapter of the book the complicity of the states is too evident to be ignored. Incidentally, Japan took the major lead. In the name of prevention of spread of epidemics in the Japanese army the hidden agenda was to investigate the utility of the biological agents for warfare. The bacteria were plague, anthrax, typhoid and cholera, the efficacy of which was tested on human beings. They had huge facility of production which could produce hundred of kilograms of these agents in the year. There is evidence to suggest that these biological weapons were used against prisoners of war. At the end of Second World War the testimony of Japanese perpetrators of these weapons resulted into their conviction and they were suitably awarded punishment by the International Military Tribunal.

South Africa, Germany and United Kingdom were not far behind and had developed the capability of producing these weapons. South Africa even constituted huge pool of scientists who were not only well paid but also brain washed to believe that their duties were patriotic activities towards their nation. UK even attempted the possibility of wiping out German beef and dairy industry by manufacturing linseed oil cakes so much so that even manufacture of these cakes was outsourced. These cakes were air dropped in grazing ground of live stock in Germany. The Americans, however, laid more emphasis to incapacitate the victim than to kill them. They believed it takes two persons and few hours to bury a dead but requires half a dozen people with some number of days (as against hour) to take care of an incapacitated individual. It appears that United States had yet some traces of moral scrupulous but the tale of Hittler killing millions of Jews in gas chambers is too ghastly event to recollect. The Russians also used biological weapons but only as tactical weapons like anthrax and bio regulators.

Iraq is the only country in the Middle East which had ambitious projects of biological weapons. The break down of USSR into numerous independent states came as a handy blessing in disguise to them. The displaced scientists from the erstwhile USSR were employed by Iraq at astronomical salaries which they could never dream of. But the projects of Iraq became an alibi to the United States to declare war on Iraq. Surprisingly the Americans did not find the existence of biological weapons but one cannot say with any degree of certainty what is the truth. We all know that the truth is the first casualty in the event of war. The recent capture of certain areas of Iraq by the Sunni insurgents called ISIS does indicate the existence of elaborate infrastructure for manufacture of the biological weapons.

Biological warfare agents are unconventional weapons and have numerous methods of delivery nevertheless these can also be delivered by conventional methods by the armed forces. They can make use of these with the help of the weapons used by them and these can be:-

(i) Aircraft system.
(ii) Artillery system.
(iii) Surface-to-surface rockets and guided missiles besides special war heads.
(iv) Infantry weapons.
(v) Surface ships and submarine.
(vi) Improvised ammunitions.

Dr Chauhan is not only theoretical in evaluation of the biological weapons but enlightens us about the demoralising consequences of suicide human bombers simulating hypothetical scenario which could become a reality considering our proximity to international borders and mushrooming of terrorist outfits in our neighbourhood. A set of terrorists infected with small pox can carry deadly anthrax spores in their hands, pockets and uniform and roam around freely in congested streets, public places, restricted and prohibited areas undetected even by metal detectors, coughing and dusting themselves with a view to inject with small pox anthrax. He takes Moga a town in Punjab where he was posted as Senior Supdt. of Police. According to his analysis, total drug requirement of doxycycline for the population of 1.5 lakhs would work out 1680 kgs. Assuming adjoining Jagraon and Faridkot cities too one affected the requirement for 3 lakhs population would be 3120 kgs. This requirement is based on an assumption that the population is already immunized and if not so already the treatment has to be carried for 60 days not 28 days which the drug requirement has been worked out and thus the total drug requirement would increase three fold. This is a scenario which constitutes a mini geographical area and a very little human population. If we take Mumbai, Delhi, Kolkata and Chennai our prophylactic response will be just to mitigate inadequate the miseries of helpless innocent citizens.

We are now facing yet another new phenomenon of effects of biological weapons which we call the agro-terrorism. Dr Chauhan evinces equal interest in agro-terrorism infected by the biological weapons. It is not difficult to find an answer to his enthusiasm. Although brought up and educated in the metro cities of India like Mumbai and Delhi he had natural interests in the landscape of the country side because he always identified his roots in the village inhabited by his grandparents. His grandfather Harpal Singh was a nominee Sub-Inspector of Police in Uttar Pradesh after he matriculated from Udai Pratap College Benares (Now Varanasi) in 1920. In those days, there was no direct recruitment of Dy. Supdt. of Police or Superintendents of Police and this was the highest entry point for any native citizen to get in to the police force. The British rulers knew the importance of the police force for sustenance of their colonial rule and always made it a point only to induct only the Rajputs and Muslims who too belonged to the Rajput Caste. Do not be surprised even the Muslims have a caste system which they did not caste off even after embracing Islam.

A very amazing incident needs mention here which reflects the enormous preponderance and the clot the police enjoyed during the British rule in the governance of the country. The incident is the part of an autobiography of a Sub-inspector of Police named Usman Ali who retired as Dy. Superintendent of Police sometimes before the independence. The auto-biography was serialised in Saptahik Hindustan, a Hindi weekly, published by Times of India Group about four decades back. The story runs like this :-

> Usman Ali appeared as a witness in a criminal case in Allahabad High Court in Civil Dress. The Hon'ble Judge who was an ICS officer did not like the audacity of police

sub-inspector and adjourned the proceeding giving directions to the police officer to re-appear again on the following day in full ceremonial dress.

Usman Ali, in full ceremonial dress, mounting, his horse with sword in hand, climbed to the chamber of the honourable judge through the stair case as his court was located on the first floor and parked himself in the witness box. The judge took a very serious view of his behaviour and reprimanded him and questioned him about his funny behaviour. Usman Ali did not reply him, dismounted from his horse and placed the police manual on his table, the relevant chapter duly flagged which prohibited an officer to open his mouth while in ceremonial dress except for giving lawful command by words of mouth. The judge mellowed down and discharge him honourably. Yes horse was a part of the ceremonial dress of a police officers in those days.

His grandfather, however, took a voluntary retirement in the year, 1947 to look after his agriculture land since they had a large land holding being zamindar of three villages in Banda district (Now Chitrakoot) in U.P. It was then a very backward district with no irrigational facilities. He purchased a diesel pump which was imported from England by the State government for sale to big land holders and embanked upon an ambitious plan of engaging himself in production of vegetables in a big way at commercial scale. In these days of early fifties these agricultural activities were undertaken by a particular caste called Kunjara Kachhi as it was below dignity for the upper caste Zamindars to engage in production of the vegetable crops. He was thus secretly but humorous conferred the title of Kunjda which he could not careless.

During the summer vacations, Dr Chauhan, as a child eagerly awaited the visit to his native village Arki as he enjoyed thrilling bullock cart races involving ten kilometers ride to his village which was the only mode of transport to reach the remote village in early seventies. Fortunately, there is no ordeal of this kind anymore as the village is accessible by tarred roads and a car can drive right upto the door step. The lush green fields of crops fascinated him. Even the cattle, like cows, buffaloes, sheep and goats amused him as these peculiar scenarios were hardly visible in the metro cities. The visit to his maternal grandfather who had settled in Shrinathpur village of Pratapgarh district after retiring as a Senior Revenue Officer also provided him the identical environment. The elders in his native village still recall with glee the prodding questions he used to ask them like holding of their land, produce of different cops per acre. These questions were raised by him when he himself did not know anything about farming and was not even in double digit of his age. The flora, fauna and the live stock in the country side always fascinated him and he could never shake off this obsession. In his periodical visits to his village, he even picked up the spoken language in the country side. His colleagues in the Police Academy were always confused to know as to which state of India he belonged to as he could speak fluently in Hindi, Marathi, English, French and Awadhi languages. It is a different matter now that his proficiency in Punjabi language may have overshadowed his fluency in dialect of Hindi and French. It is a matter of interest to know that French or German are the two foreign languages which have to be opted by the students of the secondary schools of the Maharashtra Education Board.

We diverted from the main subject only to state the reasons of his extra-ordinary interests in agricultural matters and his concern for the common man basically because he continues to be rooted in his village background. Now coming to the real subject matter which Dr Chauhan presents in the new dimensions of biological warfare in chapter five of the book, he opines that the agricultural terrorism has been the most neglected subject although it is most destructive economically, socially and politically. There appears to be no accepted definition of agro-terrorism but according to him the definition could be "use of diseases, agents against agricultural targets including crops, live stock, sea/water resources in an effort to cause widespread damage or destruction of the target with an aim to create economical, social and political class."

It is definitely a very frightening scenario even to the United States who have around one trillion dollar agro-based industry. In developing countries like India where roughly 70 per cent of the population is engaged in agriculture-related profession and one primarily depends on weather, agro terror may add to their miseries. No wonder agro terror is also called "asymmetric warfare" because it can go on unnoticed and no responsibility can be pin pointed.

The motivations and major goal of the agro-terrorism could be:-

(i) Undermine social stability and create mass panic.
(ii) Create political turmoil/upheaval.
(iii) Economic destabilisation.

The advantages of agro-terrorism to our enemies are manifold in comparison to terrorism against human targets. These could be listed as under:-

(i) Easy availability and transferability like plant fungi.
(ii) Easy to weaponise, for example, deadly foot and mouth disease. All one has to do is to scrap a lesion of an affected animal and make other victims smell it.
(iii) Easy delivery, for example, aerial spraying which can pass of as routine activity in rural areas.
(iv) Low hazard for perpetrators as it is safe for the person executing it.
(v) Lower moral guilt as no human killing is involved.
(vi) Passed as natural i.e. it can be presumed to be a natural calamity and detection is delayed.
(vii) Can be remotely done by contaminating seed products and exported to the targeted country.

(viii) Unawareness i.e. those responsible to safeguard against the calamity leave alone famous even educated functionaries have no clue about it.

(ix) Retaliation is difficult since these operations are carried out clandestinely.

(x) Most animal diseases are presumed to have been eradicated and therefore no vaccine programmes are in vogue.

(xi) Genetically modified plants have reduced assistance.

(xii) Ever after gen the outbreak several normal crops and animals have to be killed/destroyed to ensure total eradication as prophylaxes are in effective against the agro-terrorism.

For agro-terrorism, states as well non-state are to be blamed equally. The possibilities which Dr Chauhan is advancing to buttress his argument are purely hypothetical just to underline the ill consequences of the agro-terrorism. We all know that after the US, China is the largest cotton exporter in the world. They can induce fungal disease by spraying using the commercial airlines. Similarly, fine wine-makers of the European countries are equally vulnerable. Let us come closure to our own backyard. Pakistan is world's third largest producer of cotton after the USA and China. India introduces pests which destroys the Pakistans cotton crop. Pakistan too being an immediate neighbour can do the same thing to India by destroying our wheat, rice, crops in Punjab and groundnut crop in Gujarat. The non-state actors too can be employed in agro-terror activities although the scale of damage will be less if individuals are employed in such missions.

Let us see what the characteristics of anti-plant biological agents are. Few select examples are:-

(i) *Stem rust-* fungal disease which affects stem and leaves of the plant which can result in significant loss of crops.

(ii) *Sugar beet curly top virus*- it is a viral disease transmitted by beet leaf hopper an insect which can cover a large area which comes dwarfed leaves and swollen veins.

(iii) *Rice blast*- is a fungal disease causes lesions on leafs which may result in loss of 60 per cent of the crop.

(iv) *Tobacco mosaic virus*- it is a viral disease which causes stunted growth in younger plants.

A few examples of animal biological agents are:-

(i) *Aspergillum*-it is a fungal disease which affects poultry. It causes lethargy, loss of appetite and paralysis.

(ii) *Foot and mouth disease*-it is highly contagious viral disease which affects cattle, pigs, sheep and goats which has a mortality rate of over 50 per cent. It is considered the most feared animal disease. The disease causes blisters in foot and mouth which cause loss of appetite and interruption in milk production.

(iii) *Heart waler*-it is caused by a virus and affects cattle, sheep and goats which result in loss of appetite and respiratory distress and mortality rate is from 40 per cent to 100 per cent.

(iv) *New castle disease* - it is a highly contagious viral disease affecting poultry causing respiratory and nervous problems and has 100 per cent mortality role.

(v) *Cattle plague* - it is highly contagious viral disease primarily through direct contact and by drinking infected water.

All bacteria's vary in shape and size and cause disease in human beings invading host tissues or by producing toxins. The diseases they produce however can be contained as specific therapy as line of treatment have now been evolved over a period of time but there is no guarantee as such since certain germs grow even in the absence of a host cell.

All wars are horrible experiences. A society or a nation can overcome the catastrophe of a conventional war as the phenomenal development of Japan and Germany the most affected countries of Second World War would suggest. The effects of biological warfare however linger on even after the war is over. The biological weapon inflict untold misuses like hunger and disease on the helpless citizens which may take years to recover. The genesis of war on Iraq which we have commented earlier was essentially the outcome of threat Iraq posed to the world community owing to its alleged possession of biological weapons. The threat of the biological weapons is very real as these are more destructive, disruptive. It has since become more threatening owing to the use of *jihadi* militants who have their modules in roughly 70 countries of the world. Inter continental ballistic missiles with nuclear heads can be faced more effectively in comparison to the threat posed by biological weapons since there are no effective defence mechanism evolved so far.

Dr Chauhan has made gigantic efforts to identify the biological weapons, symptoms of their affect on their targets it be it a human being, plant or an animal. He has also touched upon the legislative efforts by the global political leadership to contain and eliminate the threat of biological which is as serious as a nuclear holocaust.

The work by Dr Chauhan is highly technical and definitely difficult to be really understood in its full import. However, he has made it as simple as feasible to be of value even to a disinterested reader. All said and done the human society shall always remain grateful for his efforts in bringing out the destructive potential of the biological weapons. The book shall always remain useful to the governmental heads, world health organisations, microbiologists, scientists and strategic thinkers to fight the menace posed by the biological weapons.

# Chapter XVI

# A Vital Statute at the Doorstep of Citizens in Punjabi. The Right to Information Act, 2005 along-with the Punjab Right to Information Rules, 2005

To be honest we wanted to abstain to comment on his efforts in relation to the above cited two vital statutes cited above. The reasons were two fold. Firstly, our total ignorance of the Punjabi language and secondly, our total lack of understanding the statute.

Any governmental administrative machinery thrives on secrecy and the common man who is most affected is completely in dark. In a way this work culture gives rise to corruption and also becomes a breeding ground for mushrooming of dubious middle men.

The Government of India by enacting the law on right to information and rules made thereof has really extended the helping hand to common citizen and it shall go a long way to address their grievances. The Government of Punjab took the lead and modelled on the Central statute made Right to Information Act-2005 and Right to Information Rules-2005 to fulfill the common man's aspirations.

As we are aware, the laws enacted by our legislature have a peculiar linguistic pattern which is seldom understood by common man.

Though Sharad never studied the Punjabi language in his academic career he acquired the proficiency in the written and spoken language by seer hard work and keen desire to learn.

To undertake the translation work, he preferred the Punjabi language as it is the language of the masses who are intended to be the beneficiary of the statute. We appreciate his efforts because it is no easy job to translate a statute because the letter and spirit of the translation has to conform to the original statute. Dr Sharad has done a great service to the common man by taking it to their door steps.

## Chapter XVII

# Finally the Global Recognition

In English language, the words recognised and recognition sound similar owing to their structure similar but are miles apart. Unfortunately, all human endeavours is invariably motivated by getting recognised because we construe it to be synonymous with the recognition. To get recognised is dependent on an acquired status which is transient whereas the recognition is primarily on what we contribute and what we give to the society for its growth. Thus, to get recognised one only takes benefits from the society whereas to get recognition one is blessed for only giving to the society.

George Bernard shaw, the greatest playwright of the modern English literature was once asked as to why he chose the profession of a writer and he quipped that it was the only profession in the world where even the readers of his own literary works cannot recognise him. One can walk in crumpled dress, torn shoes and no one will notice him. Little did he realise that although he could camaflauge his identity and claim anonymity but could he caste away the recognition which he would get as a writer. A genuine writer simply cannot escape the recognition. It is worth recalling an incident which took place in the late forties. All India Progressive Writers Association a leftist literary movement was holding its annual convention in Lahore. All the stalwarts of the Hindi literature were waiting outside the convention hall to welcome the

President of the Association who was to preside over the function. Munshi Prem Chand the great Hindi novelist the Hindi literature has ever produced, was incidentally the then President of the Association alights from a rickshaw in simple *dhoti* (loin cloth) and *kurta* (a loose shirt) to inaugurate the function. Nobody recognised him and poor fellow had to introduce himself and take them all inside the hall for the function to begin.

What we understand from the incident is that being recognised is a physical phenomena and is attributable to one's status either in the administrative machinery or financial status in the society and diminish in due course of time. The recognition whereas is very stable and is always empowered by one's intellectual or social contribution has a much wider acceptance and has a stamp of permanency. By being merely a writer people may fail to recognise you as a person but would definitely award you by the recognition to the contribution made by you in the field of the knowledge.

Dr Chauhan realised this truth of reality and therefore decided to lay bare the traits of his intellect by authoring numerous books which we have already discussed in the foregoing chapters and same needs no repetition. We, however would like to work that recognition is a heady wine. The more you have it becomes insatiable and ultimately leads to irrationality totally divorced from professional ethics. We saw an advertisement recently in a national daily but no one knows who inserted it on behalf of an Indian English language novelist who already enjoys world-wide recognition and readership as a writer. It was about a novel authored by the said writer very recently. We do not know the context why it was inserted or even its necessity because it may have cost much more than the price of the total sales of the novel in case all the copies were sold out immediately after publishing. What pained us whether it was ethical to do so because it tantamounted to soliciting the readership. Besides there are hundreds of talented authors who just do not get any royalty for their work. It is certainly not an even playing field as it runs detrimental to the aspirations of budding writers and stunts their natural talent and aspirations for writing. The advertisement appears to be a forerunner of a more lucrative dream since a full-length feature film is being planned on the contents of the novel.

Fortunately for us, Dr Chauhan never sought any recognition from any quarter but the intelligence authority of UK MI 5 and MI 16 directorates across the European countries across the continent took a very positive notice of his works specially of his book "Biological Weapons" which opened a floodgate of invitations to Dr Chauhan requesting him to update their law enforcing agencies engaged in the national security. Similarly, Al-Queda threat aroused vast intellectual interest and is being extensively quoted by defence strategist in their articles published in renowned journals.

There is a strange co-incidence in events which look the western intelligence authorities to take a positive notice of Dr Chauhan's contribution of his works came to the notice of Sh. P.K. Dash, an intelligence sleuth of revenue department posted in Belgium embassy who promptly had brought Dr Chauhan's contribution to the western intelligence authorities. True to his name Sh. Dash was really a dashing officer who had carefully read his works before bringing it to the notice of MI 5 Directorate dealing with counter terrorism while interacting with them. Sooner the contents of the book came to the notice of the other intelligence agencies of the European countries, INTERPOL head-quarters in France besides world health organisation who were too quick to recognise the monumental efforts of Dr Chauhan in the field of anti-terrorism.

The modern world is in the total grip of the terrorism by fundamentalist organisations. Terrorism, in modern context is no more confined to shooting down a few law enforcing personnel by laying ambush. The development of science and technology coupled with the easy way of developing terror weapons and chemicals of mass destruction now pose a serious threat to the mankind. International Police Organisation (INTERPOL) with its headquarters at Lyon in France was first to take the initiative to put a stamp of recognition on the rich contribution made by Dr Chauhan to give a new dimension to the fight the anti-terror activities by inviting him to deliver a key note address to an august gathering of 176 heads of police investigation agencies which was holding a global conference in France on fall out of the terrorism involving biological weapons. Similarly, the modern intelligentia is equally alarmed with the growing menace of geo-political violence of the Al-Queda.

An amusing incident took place during the intervening period which does need mention. International bureaucratic agencies do not strictly follow the procedure of bureaucratic protocol as obtained in India and under in their talent hunt programme address their invitations directly to the individual with whom they want to interact on the stage for their convention. The letter therefore thus to Dr Chauhan was directly addressed to him care of Interpol wing of the CBI in New Delhi as they were not sure of his latest postal address. The person handling the mail desk in Delhi thought it was a prankster's handiwork as they could never imagine a young officer of Senior Supdt. of Police rank with only a few years of service would be given the honour of addressing a global conference on terrorism. It was only after a terse reminder by the Interpol headquarters the wisdom dawned on them and with breakneck speed they got the requisite formalities of the travel and visa finalised and Dr Chauhan thus landed in France to share the podium with other distinguished speakers who were invited from USA, Australia and World Health Organisation. It is pertinent to point out that he was the only guest speaker from the Asian continent.

As pointed out earlier, the defence strategist across the numerous continents appreciated very highly the valuable contribution of Dr Chauhan and quoted from his works extensively in their articles on matters military in their reputed magazines. Our intention is not to burden the intelligent readers with the statistics on the subject but we cannot overcome the temptation of citing at least are example. During our research on the subject, we came across an article in Defence Studies published by the Routedge, Mortimer House, Mortimer Street, London, UK. The article titled "Al-Qaeda a blueprint for international terrorism in the twenty-first century? Authored by Lieutenant Commander SP Huntington Royal Navy published on line. 24th January, 2007, quotes extensively Dr Chauhan for Al-Qaeda threat in his article. To call this an article would be misnomer and the article can conveniently be classified as a mini-book. Needless to say this article is being extensively used for research, teaching and private study purposes across numerous institutions in the field of anti-terrorism.

To choose, to be an author, is a no easy profession. It calls for self-denials of ordinary pleasures of pastime, comforts and luxuries. He is expressively lonely while conceptualising a project and except for white blank sheet of paper and a pen there is none to give him company. Notwithstanding these pitfalls if one still prefers to engage is this calling it can only be an intellectual compulsion to give shape to your imagination and thoughts. The journey becomes more tough if one decides to pick-up subjects which are highly technical where you can ill afford to take any liberty with your subject. To be an author has yet another serious handicap and it pertains to the readership. Each one of us has limited access to the books because of our own linguistic deficiencies and high cost of books. Highly sophisticated works on science and technology, philosophy, statecraft and on strategic thinking may thus not be everybody's cup of tea. Our great intellectuals realised this anomaly and therefore decided to handover their wisdom through speech as well. The most ancient literature of the world, the Vedas were never in written form to begin with and were handed over to next generations by way of speech in the form of Pravachan (discourse) to their disciples and are therefore rightly called SHRUTIS (as heard) Even Lord Krishna realised the impact of speaking when he drives the great Arjun in the mid of opposing armies in the battle of Mahabharat. He finds the greatest warrior of those lines totally disoriented to the task and was trembling with fear of ensuring loss of human life and puts down his weapons. It was Lord Krishna, through his powerful speech exhorts him to get up and perform his duties. His deep philosophical analysis of life is now inherited by as which we call Gita (the song divine). Thus, we find the intellectual pursuits have been taking the written and spoken routes simultaneously to explain us the complex realities of the life. The tradition continues even till date. A British political scientist W.H. Morrer Jones in one of his speeches had opined that Nehru "rules a country of continental size and bewildering diversities with a microphone." There can be no better endorsement of the potency of the spoken word. The speech is thus an equally strong medium to ignite the spark of curiosity in an intellectual's wind.

Dr Chauhan has a very clear perspective in so far as it relates to the exploitation of these two mediums of expression and communication in the pursuit of his intellectual ambitions. No wonder he devoted his time, energy and resources to address the intellectual community by delivering his thoughts on bio-terrorism. The intellectual community across the globe also deserves our appreciation for sponsoring and facilitating suo-motu by inviting him to address and enlighten the august gathering by his thoughts on the subject of dynamics of biological threats to human civilisation.

To understand the intellectual journey of Dr Chauhan, it would be worthwhile to re-call his exploits in the undergraduate training in Medicine in University College of Medical Sciences of the Delhi University once again. He successfully graduated in Medicine (MBBS) with honours and distinction. He topped in Microbiology, preventive and social medicine, opthalmology and was declared university gold medalist in the obstetrics and gynecology. He did not sit on laurals and continued with his intellectual pursuits' with vigour and zeal after joining the Indian Police Service in preference of his selection as a Medical Officer. He earned his Master Degree on Master of Police Management from Osmania University, Hyderabad while under training in National Police Academy. He has a flair for taking on the problems head on and his topic for Master Degree for Police Administration was traffic problems of the city of Ludhiana (Punjab) and its solutions.

His contribution to understanding the biological terror and weapons with mass destruction capabilities did not go unnoticed by the Interpol. Dr Chauhan was thus invited to attend a conference on preventing bio-terrorism from 1st to 2nd March, 2005 at Lyon (France). He also participated as an expert speaker and resource person for the Interpol to train police officers and terrorism experts of Asian countries in Singapore from 27th to 29th March, 2006.

While under training in the National Police Academy besides getting Prime Minister of India baton and Home Minister of India revolver for his outstanding performance in the training, he was also awarded the following cups and trophies :-

(i) The President of India Cup for police sciences.
(ii) The Mehta Cup for studies.
(iii) Byay Shanker Memorial Trophy for proficiency in the subject of maintenance of peace and order.
(iv) KK Shah Trophy for excellence in scientific aids to investigation.
(v) Alakh Trophy for investigation.

Dr Chauhan has insatiable traits to hone his intellectual skills, no wonder, he did not stop at what he has already acquired and has got himself registered for the degree of Doctorate of Philosophy (PhD) and his topic is "Bio-terrorism and Bio-crimes in India an analytical study" from the Guru Nanak Dev University, Amritsar (India) in which he is currently engaged with rare dedication to the subject.

## Chapter XVIII

# And Miles to Go

The title of our book *"An Intellectual in Khaki"* may raise eyebrows in intellectual community and we can easily be accused of bring partisan and prejudicial against others who may be equally talented if not more. The problem with us is that our perception of an intellectual is altogether different from others. To us the primitive caveman who invented fire and brought the qualitative changes in the life style of the aboriginal human being is really one of the greatest intellectual of this planet. To us, an intellectual is the one who shares his knowledge with community at large for the common well being of one and all without any distinction, and if such an effort has been delivered at the cost of personal comforts without any hope of returns is indeed praiseworthy.

Our understanding and interpretation of the word "Intellect" is deeply influenced by a couplet in Ram Charit Manas, an epic poem authored by Tulsi Das which reads as under कीरति मतित मूति मल सोई। सुरसरि सम सब कट हित हेहि. Loosely translated it means glory, wealth and poetry should be like river Ganges which flows for the equal benefit of one and all. It may be pertinent to point out that in all civilisation of the world, poetry was the medium of transmitting wisdom. Whether it is vedic literature as communicated to us through Vedas or any other scriptures they were delivered to the society in the format of poetry. We find even Manusmriti, a treatise on Hindu law and a complicated subject like state craft by Kautilya in his Arthshastra written in the form of poetry. The invent of prose as a conduit of knowledge is latest invention and therefore the prose and poetry are synonymous to that extent knowledge is truth and therefore the great poet says सुरसरि सम सब कह हित हेहि. The poet reveals the truth and it is immaterial and irrelevant as to what format has been used. It is erroneous to assume that poetry is nothing but fantasy. It is simply a vehicle and carrier of the noble and pragmatic thoughts which moulds our outlook on the life in a way that it is beneficial to the society at large without any distinction or preferences. To us poeting and knowledge are synonymous and are the two sides of the same coin.

*Some relaxed Moments with his Daddy and Wife Vishal Singh in Customs Patrol Craft in Bombay Harbour*

But what is this knowledge? It appears that the knowledge is ultimate manifestation of the intellect after it goes through the stages of thought, vision and requisite traits before it takes shape. Thus, intellect is the seed as well as the manifestation of the knowledge. The intellect is thus potent energy bestowed to we human beings. Unfortunately, it remains dormant in most of us and cannot be harnessed even by those who posses it. It is like energy stored and concealed in a tiny atoms but it took thousands of years to understand it and make an atom bomb from it.

The intellectuality is however double sword. We have many glaring examples but would quote only few. The first is the great Ravana who because of his own misplaced wisdom and irrational thinking chose to propagate his own brand of culture culminating into total annihilation of not only of his close kith and kin but also innocent citizens. Even the Lord Rama who vanquished him acknowledged his intellectual prowess and sent his younger brother Laxman to learn something from him before he breathed his last. Yet, another example is that of Bhishma Pitamah of the Mahabharata epic who even in his thorny death bed could deliver a long surmon on good governance to Yudhister. We can understand that self-destructive thinking of Ravana emanated from his arrogance and false ego but unfortunately Bhishma was victim of his own idealism with the existing social and political realities prevailing in the family of the Kaurav dynasty. Ultimately Bhishma realised that although Yudhister was enthroned as the emperor of the whole of Aryavasta, in Actuality he was only an emperor of a cremation ground with millions of corpses around with streams of flowing blood and wails of war widows piercing the ear-drum. He was a great intellectual but owing to unfortunate circumstances his intellectuality failed him.

Then who is an intellectual? We must admit and make it clear that our interpretation of the world is totally against conventional wisdom and we have tried to give a new dimension to it, which in our view is in confronting conformings with the unforeseen realities in the present day changing social realities. We would therefore like to state that an intellectual is one who optimises the potentialities of his mind and employs such acquired capabilities not only for his own development but ensures that it is put to best use for the ultimate benefit of the society of which he is a tiny part. He is guided by a rational thinking in discharging his obligations to the society without any prejudicial thinking. Objectivity is the hall mark of his philosophy while fulfilling his social obligations.

In the light of our unconventional interpretation of the subject, a pertinent question may be raised what are the factors which are responsible for the vast intellectual gaps between the individuals. Honestly we have no answers to this vital question and have only a wild guess like others. With our limited knowledge and experience, we would however like to say that immediate suitable environment be it physical, emotional, economical, intellectual or spiritual does influence the mind of the child to evolve as an intellectual in the course of time. A small child may lack the skill of communication but his mental faculties are constantly agitating within himself. An innocent smile or a cry of a child definitely has some concealed answers to our curiosity.

Some of our intellectual friends may even contest our claim that the two individuals differ in their intellectual capabilities. They have all the rights to think so, but to cement our argument, we would like to narrate a story. There was a very poor individual with no sufficient resources to feed his family. His woes were further aggravated as his mother was blind and the wife had no issue. To get some relief from the financial miseries he engaged himself relentlessly in prayers to appease the goddess of wealth. The goddess did appear before him in person and asked him to ask for any single boon. The poor man requested the goddess to give him just twenty four hours to think about the offer. After the twenty four hours, the goddess again reappeared before him to remind him about the boon. The poor man innocently asked that he wants his mother to see her grandson having his meals with a silver spoon. The goddess Luxmi was over struck by the intelligence of the devotee and granted him the boon as it was only a single boon which he had asked. In reality he by virtue of being wide awake to the family environment back home he capitalised his intellectual capability intelligently. He infact outwitted the goddess by structuring his request in such a way that he was blessed with three boons as against the goddess of the wealth. By intellectual prowess one can definitely tame the conflicts in life.

The story which has been just narrated above, whether creation of someone's fertile imagination or otherwise, answers our questions in very clear terms. As we are aware Sharad was fully conscious of the family environment. The parents were frequenting hospitals for curing their ailments and the rising medical bills had depleted their economic resources so adversely that happenings around could not escape the attention of even a small child. His further effort to appear in All-India Medical Exam for a government job in a medical profession was also an effort in that direction because he had definite impression that his parents had no money to open a clinic or provide a suitable infrastructure to launch him as a private medical practitioner. One thing he knew for certain that by becoming a doctor he could definitely be of some help to rescue the family from the crises which was virtually because of their own making.

Yet a very interesting story as told to us needs mention since it reveals the true humane quality of Sharad. During the medical examination for being appointed as a resident medical officer in the northern railway, there was a doctor ahead of him in the queue. He had a limp in his walk. With a view to humiliate him, the eye specialist conducting the medical examination who was the medical superintendent of an eminent railway hospital spoke sarcastically by saying that as how come he could become a doctor in the railway with such pronounced limp in his walk. The humiliated doctor was rather too discreet to retort but Sharad could not digest disgusting humiliation of a fellow doctor. He jumped into the verbal spat and shot back if the limping doctor could complete his internship in a research and referred hospital of repute like All India Institute of Medical Sciences how could there be any problem for him in performing his duty in the railway department. It was an unwarranted and unsolicited intervention and did not go well with the renowned specialist. We are not aware as to what was the fate of the humiliated doctor, but out of sheer vendetta Sharad was failed in the medical test by declaring his eyes sight 6/36 as against 6/6 required for being declared fit. It was blatant misuse of authority. Sharad had no option but to secure justice for himself the review board which set aside the findings of the initial medical examination but the medical board President informed father of Sharad that if they were to state the reasons of his being declared medically unfit, the doctor who had given such a false report would himself lose his job. Such was the temperament of Sharad from the very beginning even while his own career was at stake. He could not stomach the insult and humiliation even of a person whom he had never seen, met or known in life. This is what we call being a real intellectual.

A very valid question can be raised as to how father of Sharad who was not dependent financially on anyone could land his own family in a total financial mess? The answer lies in the irrational idealism and uncontrolled emotions of his father who virtually gave away to others whatever he earned with complete disregard to his own future or personal interests. Little did he realise that such irrational populism only generates, insatiable greed in self-centred men as to why to walk or run when the life's journey can be easily completed simply by riding a some one's neck. In the midst of the ruins and misfortunes, the personality of Sharad evolved in its own unique way. He came to the conclusion that there was no short cut to skert challenges in life and academic excellence was the only way to overcome the miseries of life. The belated wisdom acquired by his parents to enhance their academic qualifications also gave Sharad not only the necessary inputs but also the resolve. He went into the shell and drowned himself in the studies- to equip himself to achieve his goals. The raising graph of his academic brilliance amply supports our opinion about his intellectual powers.

*And some relaxed moments in the Mumbai Harbour on Board Customs Patrol Craft engaged in Anti-smuggling operations.*

Choosing the path to achieve excellence is not all that easy. It is definitely not a pleasant walk in a rose garden. There are innumerable obstacles to deflect you from your mission. Social environment, temptations of comfortable life can any time throw you out of the trajectory leading to your goal. It definitely requires tremendous will power, austerity and intellectual intensity to stay on a steady course. Unless one renunciates his physical comforts and proceeds with a single mindedness and diligence dreams can remain only a wishful thinking.

Nature expresses itself in an infinite vast expanse. Mind too is nothing but a mini replica of this vast nature stored in the hard disc of our brain. If we interfere with its inherent benevolent qualities we can never escape the fury our own mind. There is a true incident which needs to be shared. When Nadir Shah, a foreign invader, landed Delhi, he resorted to indiscreet loot and carnage of its citizens. Intelligentia of the city was greatly pained and approached him to show mercy to the helpless citizens by going around giving public an assurance to that he will call of often brutal killing. He conceded the request of the respected citizens of the city and mounted an elephant offered to him go around. After mounting the elephant he asked for the Nakel (a rope passing through the nostrils of the animal) for keeping the animal under control himself. Infact, our mind is certainly like a wild elephant and can go berserk, if left uncontrolled. Not an easy task as we all know and witness every day in our life.

Yet another factor which contributes to our intellectual growth is the time factor like nature, it is also vast and infinite. It has neither a beginning nor an end since it is available to us in abundance and is free of cost. Its importance and value has been rather been never understood. Ultimately we run short of time and blame this for which we alone are accountable. We take refuse behind false pretexts claiming that the time has been very cruel to us or time has gone against us. In reality, the time is very friendly and kind to us, it is we who have never understood its importance. We have our own erroneous calculations that things can be achieved at leisure and time becomes the first casualty of our negligence and simultaneously we become a living example of non-performance. Sharad recognised the importance of time. It is not that he was only a book worm. He was equally mischievous, playful and had enough sense of humour to become a pleasing companion to his playmates. The intellectual traits were however always visible and not too difficult to understand. To quote an example his *tauji* (father's elder brother) was flabbergasted when Sharad hardly of four years of age asked him as to how much agricultural land was owned by the family. Any body would be.

My co-author narrates a very enlightened conversation which Sharad had with a visiting relative where she was also present on the occasion. The visiting relation a qualified aeronautical engineer well placed in her career in the Indian Air Force asked a very probing question as to why he had given up a bright medical career with his enviable track record in the medical studies. Without much thought to the question Sharad instantly replied that a doctors name, frame and money flowed in direct proportion to the persons falling sick and thus a doctor is useful only to the sick citizens beyond that his excellence has no relevance. He, however, added further that he still continues to perform the same job. As a police officer he is definitely engaged to promote and maintain the social and ethical health of the society.

We recollect having read long age somewhere that the word constable is derived from the word console. We are, however, in no position to substantiate it at this point of time. The vocabulary of the English language has essentially developed by uses and borrowing liberally from the numerous European languages unlike our Indian languages which owe their origin to the Sanskrit language and virtually every word of it has a root to which it traces its origin. In case it is really proved that the word constable traces it origin from the word console, it only confirms that whosoever attributed such meaning was really a genuine friend of the society.

Policing is the most visible face of the governance and covers each and every individual, high or low in the social order or hierarchy. The process of law and wheel of justice gets into motion invariably from a police station. It is however also a fact that it is the most maligned organ of the administrative machinery. Partly we all are equally to be blamed because we also harbour prejudices against them for no justifiable reasons.

Gone are the days when the first Prime Minister of India could easily go to his office in south block of the secretariat or for that matter to any place in Delhi or elsewhere in India. There were no road clearances, no cavalcade of their security vehicles or ambulances in tow. It was really a pleasant sight when he moved around in his ambassador car escorted by a lone police officer riding his motor cycle ahead of him. The current generation born after the seventh decade of the century may not believe it to be true. This fact needed recapitulation because the ground realities today are entirely different. The character of policing duties has multiplied manifold resulting into avoidable ill consequences.

The ratio of the police force and the population is very dismal in India in comparison to the developed countries. In modern scenario as we see at least one-third districts of India are engulfed in the Maoist violence which further affects their sagging morale. The weaponry which they have to rely upon is definitely inferior to the weapons in possession of Maoists to carry out their nefarious activities. No wonder the casualties of police forces in a year are as high as the battle casualties of our military forces in any single war which we were forced upon to fight by our enemies. Be it rain or storm freezing cold or scorching heat the police man is out there on duty for us. It is not that we hold a brief for them but he is an integral part of our society which we have created for ourselves. It is unfortunate that just because he is too visible to us he is singled out for the undue criticism and condemnation. We seldom appreciate or applaud him for his good works. There are definitely black sheep everywhere in any set up as we have no access to the closed door happenings elsewhere we must equally shore the blame after all we can only see only our face in the mirror and not that of the neighbour next door.

We tried to study the problem our own way and analyse the anomaly to arrive at a fair and sound judgment. The best way was to locate and cultivate such individual as our informer who could provide unbiased assessment of the force. To our luck we did find such an individual who was willing to speak. We shall not disclose the identity of the person since informers all over the world enjoy absolute immunity against their exposive. The informer so cultivated had virtually the experience of working in a reputed intelligence organisations where they had to be heavily dependent on the co-operation of the state police forces in various states. The operations of the intelligence organisation necessitated enthused overt operations all over India not only in cities but also in the remote village areas affected by insurgencies. In all these operations, the local police were employed to assist the overt operations. The informer could not re-call even a single incident which could point out to any dereliction of duty or leakage of information to the targeted individuals or syndicates by the police personnel associated with the task notwithstanding the fact that the monetary inducements were very interative. We do not deny the observations of the society which we witness in our day-to-day with the police departments but at best these can be taken as an exception which equally afflicts the other departments of the government.

In war times we came across very inspiring phrases like "raw courage" "beyond the call of duty" or supreme sacrifice in citations of the soldiers in recommendations for their gallantry awards. Why cannot we imbibe these virtues in our own professional walks of life to enable the fellow citizens to get inspired from our conduct? Unfortunately we are too embroiled in pursuits of our own materialistic displacements in our life.

Sharad was a privy to an incident in the formative years of his grooming in the police department which must have left a deep imprint in his mind. The true story runs like this:-

It was sometimes in August, 1999, the sea was at its maximum fury in Bombay harbour. It was raining heavily and the high sea tide resulted in high waves just to make it extremely risky to venture out at sea. Father of Sharad was holding a very high and responsible post in Mumbai. Preventive commissionerate at that time when an young helpless lady who was the liaison officer of the Brazilian Embassy in Mumbai walked in. It so happened that a Brazilian cargo ship with sixteen crew members had collided with a rock and grounded at sea off the Bombay harbour and was listing dangerously with imminent possibility of sinking along-with the crew. She had found no helpful response from any other local agency to rescue the precious human life. Even the helicopter of the Pawanhans attached to Bombay Preventive Commissionrate refused to take off in such a hazardous weather.

After taking the due permission from the supervisory officer who consented positively to undertake the rescue measures the custom team proceeded towards the site where the tragedy was looming large to happen. The customs patrol craft of Norwaygian built although very robust was dancing on the sea waves like a tennis ball in a hard court. After a sustained and breathtaking effort, all the crew members were brought to the shore. Smile of gratitude of the crew members was sufficient to forget the risk of the hazardous and risky operation. The ship however embraced the watery grave later.

In due course, the Brazilian ambassador in Delhi flew down to Bombay and threw a grand cocktail party to express his gratitude to the officers engaged in the rescue operation. The invitees included city's who's who besides the senior officers of the customs commissionrate. When the entire invited guest had left, the ambassador requested father of Sharad to give him company for a drink of old monk rum for the road. What we want to impress is that the foreign diplomats do a lot of home work to know the preferences of their guest in a host country. He had perforce served the precious single malt whiskeys in the function keeping in view the high profile guests but he knew for certain that the party would be incomplete if he did not offer a peg of rum with his real chief guest. In Bombay preventive commissionrate a bottle of old monk rum is code-named a coconut and offer of such pure healthy drink is seldom refused. The incident was narrated to Sharad on telephone by his mother and needless to say he gave a liberal dressing down to his father unmindful that he himself was performing such duties day in and day out which also could be constrained to be beyond the call of duty.

Ordinarily we perceive an individual to be an intellectual if he is highly read and capable of articulating his wisdom in the choosen field of his studies or activities. But to us such a narrow interpretation lacks universal applicability. An outstanding scientist may be a utter failure in the field of administration. A genius in the field of musicology may not understand what the theory of relatively talks about. A brilliant military strategist may be a very successful campaigner in war but he may acquit himself very poorly in other spheres of human activities. To explain our perception more clearly we would like to give only two examples. Sigmund frend, a German philosopher, who propounded the theory of incestuous relationship is considered a revolutionary thinker in the field of sexual behaviours. But it is sage Manu who warns us in Manusmriti, a treatise on human law that a mother and his son or father or his daughter should not stay in darkness and in an isolated place together. Similarly, Karl Marx in his Das Capital talks of the equality of wealth, which definitely had huge impact on political thoughts in the twentieth century but we forget that our thinkers gave us the concept of *Vasudhaiv Kutumbkarn* (Universal brotherhood). It needs no effort to explain that in a family, all members enjoy equal rights to the wealth. To us intellectual is the one who not only identifies a problem but also offers a pragmatic solution to enhance the quality of our life. It therefore appears to us that we should evaluate the entire personality of an individual to consider him to be an intellectual. The broad parameters which we have stipulated to be the touch stone for an individual to be called an intellectual could be spelt as under:-

(i) Capability to understand the influences of environment be it social, political or of any other kind.

(ii) Enunciate a course of action or actionable strategy to overcome the adverse impacts of the environment.

(iii) To develop an invincible spirit to fight the challenges of life in the face of hardships and hurdles.

(iv) To constantly engage himself to improve upon the academic excellence to broaden his understanding and vision of life.

(v) To honour the value of the time by way of efficient time management to achieve the goals set for ownself.

(vi) To be honest and transparent in speech, thought and actions while dealing with sub-ordinates or common citizens.

Owing to our myopic vision, we all see nature as an inanimate object. It is far from true. We fail to perceive the message which the nature conveys to us to understand the tune meaning of the life. The river Ganges flows uninterruptedly and mountains cannot block its way to flow and thus it creates a fertile basin for the growth of civilisation. The incessant dancing waves of the sea convey us the unambiguous message of constant endeavour. The infinite sky over our head guides us to think big and vast.

The purpose of our humble effort to pen the short biography of the police officer in question was primarily with a view because we found the young and ambitious generation had something to emulate from his towering and still evolving personality. Since we are witness of his journey from the very close quarters we found ourselves competent of undertaking the job. And in no way we are overawed by his personality or achievements because according to us it is an evolving phenomenon. We hope our mini effort of authoring this short biography would always motivate him to acquit himself with greater excellence and would also be of immense value to aspiring youth of our great nation.

Teachers by nature and temperament are prone to offer unsolicited advice and how could we behave otherwise? We would therefore conclude our humble effort by advising Sharad quoting a couplet from Ram Charit Manas by great poet Tulsi Das.

जड़ चेतन गुन दोषमय, विश्व कीन्ह करतार।
संत हंस गुन गहहि पय, परिहरि वारि विकार।।